WHAT WE BELIEVE
LEADER'S GUIDE • PART 2
SECOND EDITION

CRC Publications
Grand Rapids, Michigan

Unless otherwise indicated, the Scripture quotations in this publication are from the HOLY BIBLE, NEW INTERNATIONAL VERSION, © 1973, 1978, 1984, International Bible Society. Used by permission of Zondervan Bible Publishers.

Cover photo: SW Productions/PhotoDisc

What We Believe (Leader's Guide), © 1988, 2000 CRC Publications, 2850 Kalamazoo Ave. SE, Grand Rapids, MI 49560. All rights reserved. With the exception of brief excerpts for review purposes, no part of this book may be reproduced in any manner whatsoever without written permission from the publisher. Printed in the United States of America on recycled paper. ⊕

We welcome your comments. Call us at 1-800-333-8300 or e-mail us at editors@crcpublications.org.

ISBN 1-56212-528-1

10 9 8 7 6 5 4 3 2 1

Contents

Introduction 5

Session 13 Jesus Christ (1) 9

Session 14 Jesus Christ (2) 15

Session 15 The Church (1) 21

Session 16 The Church (2) 27

Session 17 Sacraments: Baptism 33

Session 18 Sacraments: The Lord's Supper 39

Session 19 Dispensationalism 45

Session 20 End Times: Premillennialism 53

Session 21 End Times: The Reformed View 59

Session 22 Being Distinctively Reformed 67

Session 23 Living as a Christian 75

Session 24 Profession of Faith/Recommitment 83

Introduction

You are reading the leader's guide to Part Two (sessions 13-24) of a twenty-four–session video course entitled *What We Believe.*

When we first produced *What We Believe* back in 1988, we thought it would serve the churches well for perhaps five years or so. To our delight, demand for the course far surpassed our predictions and remains strong today. Thousands of students and many leaders have watched the video and used these materials to learn or review the basics of our faith.

In response to numerous requests to "update" this popular course, CRC Publications, with the help of Back to God Hour television, persuaded Rev. Lew Vander Meer to re-shoot the video. We've added many fresh ideas and examples as well as a number of scenes shot outside the studio. We've revised this leader's guide, adding leader tips, options, and a number of new discussion questions. The student session guides, originally written by Curt Walters, were also revised.

FORMAT AND AUDIENCE

This twenty-four–session course teaches students in grades nine through twelve the basics of the Christian faith according to the Reformed/Presbyterian tradition. Although this is not a course on the Belgic Confession, the sessions basically follow its sequence and frequently refer to its articles (if the Belgic is not part of your confessional tradition, you can omit referring to it during the discussion part of the course).

Each session in this course features a twenty-minute video presentation by Rev. Lew Vander Meer, a veteran high school Bible teacher and pastor. After each video presentation, students use a handout to review key facts, discuss issues raised by the video, and apply the teachings to their lives.

What We Believe may be adapted to various patterns of use. For example, some groups might want to use all twenty-four sessions in sequence in a single year; other groups may prefer to use twelve sessions one year and twelve the following year; still others might take a breather after a dozen sessions, study some other nondoctrinal material for a few weeks, then return to study the remaining twelve sessions. Adjust your own use of these materials to your schedule and to the reactions you hear from your students.

GOALS OF THE COURSE

What We Believe is designed to

- encourage young people to make a commitment to Christ as their personal Savior and Lord.

- help young people understand the systematic structure of Reformed doctrine and enable them to acquire and use a basic "faith vocabulary" common to the Reformed/Presbyterian tradition.

- help young people appreciate the Reformed/Presbyterian tradition of Christianity in comparison with other traditions.

- enable teens to see a clear connection between doctrine and life and to respond positively to the teachings of the church.

SESSION GUIDES

A set of twelve revised session guides accompanies each of the two parts of *What We Believe.* The session guides should be torn from the perforated booklet and distributed to the students at the beginning of each session before the video segment is shown. After each session, encourage your students to save their session guides as a summary of the main teachings of the church. (You may want to provide a two-pocket folder as something of an incentive for doing so.) No homework is required or suggested for this course.

Beginning with session 14, each session guide includes a review quiz designed to help students recall key ideas from previous sessions. The quizzes focus primarily on the previous week's video but also include questions on earlier sessions (in Part Two only). Answers to all quizzes are given in this guide.

Session guides also include a space for answers to the Bible Trivia questions Pastor Lew asks on the video (evaluations of the original course show that students really enjoyed these questions). Your students can check their own answers against those given by Pastor Lew at the end of each video presentation.

The section called "Video Discussion Guide" offers questions and other activities that review key facts from the video, raise issues for discussion, and draw practical applications. You will need to determine how many of these questions you can handle in your allotted time. We encourage you to supplement (or occasionally replace) our questions with your own or those of your students.

You may want to provide copies of the Belgic Confession for your group; the video refers to and quotes from specific articles of this confession. If you plan to incorporate these references into your discussion of the video, it would be helpful to have at least one copy for every two students. You'll find the Belgic Confession in the back of the *Psalter Hymnal*. It's also available in simple booklet form from CRC Publications.

If your denomination does not use the Belgic Confession, you may, of course, choose not to discuss it during your class sessions. Most of the print references to the Belgic Confession are by way of options that you may decide not to use.

LEADER'S MATERIALS

To lead Part Two of this course, you will need the two videocassettes containing sessions 13-24.

One of the advantages of a video course is that a trained teacher and theologian comes into your classroom each week. Pastor Lew presents Christian doctrine in a way that's both clear and appealing to young people.

Each video presentation is about twenty minutes long. (If at all possible, watch the video presentations at home before viewing them with your class). We suggest at least another thirty minutes for the review quiz and the discussion of the video. An hour for the entire session would be ideal.

Discussing the video is a crucial part of this course. It gives the students a chance to interact with a knowledgeable leader, to clarify information, to discuss issues, to ask their own questions, and to draw personal applications. You don't need to be a theologian or a professional teacher to lead the discussion, but you do need to be a committed Christian who enjoys young people and who understands what the Bible and the church teach.

This leader's guide will help you through each class session. Each session includes Scripture and Belgic Confession references and a statement of purpose that summarizes the video and gives you general and specific goals for the session.

The Perspective section offers additional biblical, historical, and theological insights into the content of the session. Dr. M. Eugene Osterhaven, a retired professor of systematic theology at Western Theological Seminary, Holland, Michigan, wrote these excellent backgrounds for the original course, and we have retained them for this second edition (Robert DeMoor wrote the background for session 16). We suggest you read and reflect on this section before getting into the session procedures.

The Procedure section provides step-by-step directions for achieving the session's purpose. In it you will find answers to the review quizzes, a guide to presenting each video (we suggest stopping some videos at various points for discussion), and answers to the questions asked in the student session guides. Suggestions for group work, discussion of case studies, personal application, and other learning activities are included. The Closing section of each session presents a variety of group and personal worship options.

VARIETY

Perhaps you're wondering if twelve (or more) video presentations and discussions will have enough variety to hold the interest of active young people.

As we mentioned earlier, you needn't go through all twenty-four sessions in sequence. Any format gets boring if overworked. And, of course, some students and some entire groups may simply tune out of the video for a variety of reasons. However, our experience with the original edition of *What We Believe* strongly suggests to us that the course not only works—it works well.

Remember that the videos are only about twenty minutes long, feature a gifted communicator, and are directed especially to young people. Following the video, your own discussion time can be lively and varied. Notice too that the questions go beyond facts. Case studies, group work, and a variety of opportunities for personal application should help hold the group's interest. And we've included many creative options that take you beyond the basic questions in the session guide.

As a leader you can use your own creative approaches to inject still more variety into the sessions, if needed. Here are a few ideas:

- Turn off the video and give your own lecture to the class or help the students discover the main idea directly from Scripture and the Belgic Confession.

- Have students compete in teams on the review quiz and the Bible Trivia. Use small groups to work on the questions.

- Ask a pair of students to lead the class discussion for a session.

- Appoint pairs of students to design the concluding worship activities.

- Invite a guest speaker into your classroom.

- Take a field trip to a neighboring church that's markedly different from your own congregation.

HOME CLASSROOMS

If it's practical, try meeting with your students in your home. Young people are more likely to be relaxed and open when gathered around a television set in your family room than seated in rows of folding chairs in church. You can ask students to take turns bringing refreshments.

Teaching in your home does cut down class size to perhaps a dozen or less, but a small group is great for interacting and really getting to know each other.

EVALUATION

We welcome your comments on this course. Please contact us at 1-800-333-8300 or e-mail us at editors@crcpublications.org. Thank you.

CRC Publications Staff

Jesus Christ (1)

SCRIPTURE

Genesis 1:1-2; Matthew 1:20-23; 28:18; John 1:1, 14; 14:6-7; 20:31; Philippians 2:5-11

BELGIC CONFESSION

Article 18

PURPOSE

Today's video marks the beginning of Part Two of this course (your class should have already taken Part One, sessions 1-12). Today's session looks at the person of Christ; next week's session focuses on the atoning work of Christ. Pastor Lew begins by discussing the incarnation and the virgin birth. Citing John 1:1, 14 and Article 18, he defines the incarnation as God taking on human flesh. Just as the world was originally formed by the action of God, so Jesus was formed by the action of God in the womb of Mary. As a result, Jesus is both real God and real man, of the same essence with the Father, yet human like us. The names of our Lord (Jesus, Immanuel, Messiah, Christ, "bread of life") help us understand who he is. Pastor Lew then goes off the set into a bakery to explain how Jesus is the bread of life. The video concludes with comments on how Jesus is our link to God.

After today's session, your students should be able to evaluate their own relationship to Jesus Christ, the God-man who loves them. They should be able to describe the incarnation, the virgin birth, and the various names given to Christ (see above). They should be able to explain how Christ is the bread of life and how he is our link to God.

PERSPECTIVE

In our study of Jesus Christ, we touch the heart of our faith, that to which the Old Testament leads and from which the New Testament flows. Jesus Christ is indeed the center of God's special revelation, the key to a proper understanding of both testaments (Luke 24:44; John 5:39; Acts 3:24; Heb. 1). In him God became one of us. Previously, God had sent his word in one form or another; now the Word *himself*—not itself—appeared. What is the Word of God? A verbal symbol, a prophetic message, paper and ink? In its highest form it is a person, the Word incarnate, or "the Person of the speaking God," as John Calvin calls that Word (*Institutes*, 1, 7, 4). "In Christ all the fullness of the Deity lives in bodily form" (Col. 2:9). This is the good news; this is the heart of Christianity.

It is little wonder, then, that the Belgic Confession devotes five full articles (10, 18-21) and parts of others to the person and work of Christ. In this session we deal with his incarnation and identity as God and man; in the next, we'll look closely at his two natures and at his atoning work. Article 18 begins with the fulfillment of prophecy in Christ, reminding us of the messianic expectation. This expectation, based on scores of Old Testament passages and their fulfillment in the Lord Jesus, is one of the greatest phenomena in history, second only to the fact of his coming.

The New Testament indicates that from the beginning there were those who denied that Jesus Christ was divine, and we know from other sources that before the end of the first century some were claiming that his humanity was unreal. A Jewish sect on the fringe of the church said that Jesus was the natural son of both Joseph and Mary, who was rewarded for piety by God's Spirit at his baptism. Thus qualified for messiahship, he was put to death; but he arose, ascended, and some day will return to reign on earth. Another early group believed in the virgin birth and messianic mission of Jesus but denied his eternity with the Father.

These were harbingers of a more serious error embraced by Paul of Samosata, the bishop of Antioch in the mid-third century. He held that Mary bore a "mere man" who was anointed with the Holy Spirit at his baptism, was kept from sin, "advanced" to Godhead as the Father endowed him with divine attributes, and was made the Savior of mankind: "From man he became God."

Thoughtful people in the church asked: Can Godhead be conferred or begin in time? If so, have we more than one god, like the heathen?

Before these ideas rocked the church, opposite opinions had appeared, denying Christ's true humanity. Those influenced by Greek dualism, which held that matter is evil and is opposed to spirit, claimed that Jesus had a phantom body and that his suffering too was unreal. This latter idea was based on the Greek notion that suffering is imposed from without; since no one can impose anything on the gods, the gods cannot suffer. Later, some Reformed theologians also held this idea, claiming that our Lord suffered only in his human nature.

The denial of the incarnation was refuted by the church already in the writings of the apostle John (1 John 4:11ff.; 2:22; 2 John 7; John 1:14). Throughout the second century, proclaiming the true humanity of the Savior continued to be a major concern of the church. The reason for its insistence that Christ is both God and man is the teaching of the Bible and the confession (Article 19) that he had to be both in order to make atonement and to conquer death as our representative (cf. Heidelberg Catechism, Q&A 16, 17).

Serious challenges to the church's official teaching on the nature of Christ continued into the fifth century. Arius was typical of those who believed that God is too aloof to enter creation and in so doing make himself subject to change. He dwells "alone ingenerate, alone eternal, alone without beginning, alone true, alone possessing immutability, alone wise, alone good, alone sovereign, alone judge of all." Who then is Jesus? A creature who could not comprehend the mind of the Father, since there is distance between creation, including Jesus, and God. Arius believed that it was not God who came into our world but another creature, like us and yet unlike us. Jesus' soul was unlike ours. Hence he was neither God nor man.

The church responded that if Arius was right, God, whom we worship, is not eternal; baptism is in the name of a creature; the Father was not always Father (for there was a time when he had no son); we worship a creature, Christ; we lose our Savior; and Christianity admits polytheism, the addition of gods.

Other heresies confronting the church concerned the relation of the two natures to each other and the one person of Jesus Christ (Pastor Lew goes into some of these next time). Are the two natures alongside each other without real union in one person? Is Christ's humanity lost in his divinity like a drop of honey in the ocean? Are the two natures mixed so that we have "a third something," as some have said? Who was Mary's son, a mere man or God? These were the questions facing the church. It is instructive and comforting to know that they were considered at Nicea, Ephesus, Chalcedon, and in the minds of thousands of believers, for the same questions are being asked today, and, as then, they must be answered.

PROCEDURE

Review Quiz
Normally we suggest opening each session with a review quiz; however, since your group, like many others, may have taken a fairly long break between Part One (sessions 1-12) and Part Two (sessions 13-24), no review quiz is included in today's session (your students won't mind!). The review quizzes start again next time. As in sessions 1-12, the quizzes are cumulative; that is, the review quiz for session 16 will include several questions from sessions 13-15 (but nothing from Part One).

Video Presentation
Before showing today's video, take a couple of minutes to ask students to do some thinking about the person of Jesus Christ. Ask students to give a descriptive word or title that comes to mind when they think of Christ. Go around your group two or three times so that you'll end up with a large list of words (on your board or newsprint). More than likely at least some of the words the students mentioned will be included in this or next week's session.

Explain that today's session focuses on the person of Jesus Christ. We are going to look at who Jesus is. Next week we'll focus more on what Jesus does for us and how he is able to do that. Show the video through without stopping.

Video Discussion Guide
1. What does the word *incarnation* mean as it applies to Jesus (see John 1:1, 14)? Why is the incarnation so important to Christians?

The word *incarnation* means "in the flesh." It refers to the way God came in the flesh to this world and lived for a brief time among us.

> **OPTION**
>
> Jesus Christ has been the subject of artists throughout the centuries. If you have time, pay a visit to your local library for some examples of both classical and contemporary portraits of Christ. Other good sources are the articles about Jesus that occasionally appear in national newsmagazines like *Time* and *Macleans*. When you've obtained, say, half a dozen or so portraits, show them to your students and talk about the way various artists see Christ (for example, some may emphasize his divinity, his holiness, his piety; others may show more of his humanity, his compassion, his suffering). Use the portraits (and perhaps some comments from recent magazine articles) to raise the question of who Jesus really is.

When you talk about the importance of this term for Christians, have students read John 1:1, 14. John first establishes that the Word (that is, Jesus) was God. Then, says John, this Word, this God "became flesh and made his dwelling among us." This is the basis for the key Christian teaching that Jesus is at once truly God and truly human. Next week we'll look at why this teaching is so basic to Christ's atoning work for us.

2. **Read Genesis 1:1-2 and Matthew 1:20. How is the work of the Spirit at creation similar to the work of the Spirit in the incarnation? Why is believing in the virgin birth of Jesus important?**

   As Pastor Lew says in today's video, in both Genesis and Matthew the creative power of God—expressed through the Spirit—is at work, making things out of nothing. The "emptiness" of earth at creation can be compared with the "emptiness" of Mary's womb. In the beginning the creative work of God filled the earth with life. In the incarnation, the creative work of God in Mary's womb created a God-man called Jesus.

   This "virgin birth" is very important to Christians. In fact, you may want to mention that every time we say the Apostles' Creed we confess this doctrine ("conceived by the Holy Spirit, born of the virgin Mary"). Why is this important to Christians? Because the virgin birth means that Jesus retained his divine nature while taking on our human nature. He is at once truly God and truly human. Had Jesus been born of a natural, human father, he would not have been truly God but would have inherited Mary's sinful human nature. The Spirit's creative work in Mary's womb makes Jesus an extension of God the Father—that is, real God, of the same essence as God. At the same time, his being born of a woman makes Jesus truly human. Next week we'll look at why Christ had to be both human and divine in order to atone for our sins.

3. **Tell what the following names mean:**

   - **Jesus (see Matthew 1:21):** Jesus means Savior: "You are to give him the name Jesus, because he will save his people from their sins."

   - **Immanuel (see Matthew 1:23):** Immanuel means "God with us."

   - **Christ (see John 20:31):** Christ means "anointed one." To be anointed is to be set apart by God for a unique work. The Old Testament word for "anointed one" is Messiah. Recall how Christ functions as our prophet (tells us the will of God), as our priest (offers himself as the sacrifice for our sins), and as our King (rules over all). You may also want to add that another common name for Jesus, not mentioned on the video, is "Lord," that is, the one to whom all authority on heaven and earth has been given (see Matthew 28:18).

4. **In what general way is Jesus "the bread of life"? Also, recall the specific symbolism that Pastor Lew sees in the water, flour, sugar, oil, salt, and yeast that go into a loaf of bread.**

OPTION

Distribute and read Article 18 of the Belgic Confession (quoted in part on the video) as a summary of the first two discussion questions.

TIP

Students who aren't familiar with the Bible often make the assumption that Christ is simply Jesus' last name: Jesus *Christ*. You may want to mention this when talking about the distinct meanings of the names *Jesus* and *Christ*.

OPTION

Talk about some of the other names or titles for Jesus that your students listed at the beginning of today's session.

Bread is everything we need to stay alive. Christ is our bread of life because he gives us everything necessary for life. As bread is broken to feed and nourish us, so Christ's broken body gives us life. That's the main symbolism of the bread that we break every time we take communion.

More specifically, Pastor Lew sees the water in bread as a symbol of the way Jesus cleanses us from our sin. Like seeds of wheat, Jesus dies and rises again to give us life. Like sugar, Jesus brings flavor and joy into our lives. Like oil, Jesus heals us through his Spirit. Following Jesus' example, we are to be the salt (preservative) of the world. Like yeast, we are to penetrate every part of the world and give it life through Jesus Christ.

5. **What does Pastor Lew mean when he says, "Jesus is the way we see God?" See also John 14:6-7. What qualities of Jesus help you understand—and draw closer to—God the Father?**

   Jesus said, "No one comes to the Father except through me. If you really knew me, you would know my Father" (John 14:6). Because Jesus *is* God in the flesh, we can see God most clearly in him, someone who was much like us in so many ways.

   On the second half of the question, give students a moment to think of a response. Then go around the circle and invite them to tell which qualities of Jesus (for example, his compassion for people, his humility, his power, his love) help them understand and draw closer to God the Father.

6. **Reflect for a minute or two on who Jesus is to you (reading Philippians 2:5-11 may be helpful). Then complete this statement: "Jesus, to me you are . . ."**

   You may want to read the Philippians passage aloud to the class. But tell the group that they need not restrict themselves to that passage when completing the statement.

Closing

Invite those students who wish to do so to read their statements about Jesus aloud as prayers to Jesus.

> **TIP**
> Encourage students to use their own words to complete the statement. More important, ask them to be honest as to where they are in their personal relationship with Jesus. If Jesus is someone they are just getting to know, or someone who asks hard things of them, or someone who they don't really understand, they should say so, rather than simply write something they think they should say.

> **OPTION**
> Divide into two groups and read Philippians 2:5-11 responsively. Then close with a time of silent prayer in which each student can thank God for the gift of his Son.

WHAT WE BELIEVE
SESSION 14

Jesus Christ (2)

SCRIPTURE
Matthew 27:32-54

BELGIC CONFESSION
Articles 19 and 21

PURPOSE
Last week Pastor Lew discussed the person and identity of Christ. In today's video he focuses on the atoning work of Christ. That work required that Christ have both a human and divine nature in one person, as described by Article 19. The early church established that the two natures were not separate, were not indistinguishable, but were connected, yet distinct, like intertwined forks. Christ had to be human in order to suffer for our sins; he had to be divine in order to endure that suffering. Both his humiliation and exaltation illustrate the interacting of the two natures. By suffering and dying in our place (vicarious atonement), Christ paid the price for our sins; as a result, God now finds us not guilty. Unlike our first parents, who failed to keep the covenant of works, Christ obeyed God perfectly. That perfection is now imputed to us so that we appear as perfect before God.

After today's session, your students should have a better understanding of—and a deeper sense of gratitude for—Christ's atonement for our sins. They should be able to explain the relationship between Christ's two natures and why they are necessary, define the atonement and how Christ makes us right with God, tell how Christ succeeded where our first parents failed, and say what the atonement means to them personally.

PERSPECTIVE
People sometimes speak of a certain teaching—like the incarnation or atonement—as crucial. They are saying more than they intend or realize. The word *crucial* comes from the Latin word for cross. The central importance of the cross in Christian faith has so shaped our language that anything truly important we now call crucial.

To understand the true meaning of Christ's crucial atonement work, the early church searched for images or comparisons from everyday life that would help them feel and grasp its significance One such image was based on the common experience of ransoming people from captivity and slavery. Following Jesus' own words, "The Son of Man [came] . . . to give his life as a ransom for many" (Mark 10:45), some Christians pictured Jesus' work as ransoming captives, perhaps even ransoming them from the devil's bondage. The devil, they reasoned, was willing to trade the souls of the saved for Christ's soul, a greater prize; but the devil could not hold Christ. They debated whether the devil deceived himself or was deceived by God. Others felt it was unworthy to conceive of God as dealing with the devil. They looked for other images.

One of the most important of these alternate images was developed by a man called Anselm. Influenced by his medieval environment, Anselm thought of God as a gentleman to whom honor and duty were of paramount importance. God's honor requires, he said, that "every wish of a rational creature should be subject to the will of God." Anything less is sin. If a single sin goes unpunished, God is not doing his duty as King. This would be "unbecoming" to God, for whom "even the smallest unfitness is impossible." In other words, God's honor requires that every sin be punished and every debt paid. God's justice must be satisfied; God cannot deny himself.

Future obedience does not pay for past debt; yet that debt must be paid. Who then can pay? No mere creature, even though the creature *must* pay because the creature has sinned. Only God can settle the debt, and he must do it in a human nature. "His death outweighs the number and greatness of all sins." Thus God himself satisfies his own honor and makes salvation possible.

Anselm's picturing of the atonement in terms of divine honor emphasized God's nature, the gravity of sin, and the necessity of the atonement. The reformers, although their own understanding was more in terms of holiness and justice than of honor, learned much from Anselm.

In its teaching about the atonement, the Belgic Confession emphasizes yet another image, that of priestly sacrifice. Sacrifice was central to Old Testament worship: the priests offered sacrifices to atone for the sins of the people. When these sacrifices were offered according to God's commands, the people's sins were forgiven (Lev. 4:26, 31, 35). These priestly sacrifices pointed forward to the atonement God was to offer once for all time.

Jesus Christ became that sacrifice, the "Lamb of God, who takes away the sin of the world" (John 1:29). In his priestly function, Jesus is compared to Melchizedek, the priest-king who received tithes from Abraham (Ps. 110:4; Heb. 6:20). This comparison helped the Jewish audience understand the special quality of Jesus' priesthood. Jesus was no ordinary priest—he was both priest and sacrifice; by entering "the Most Holy Place once for all by his own blood," he "obtained eternal redemption" (Heb. 9:12).

In their study of the atonement, your students are faced again with crucial questions about the nature of God. What is God like? The Bible says God is loving and merciful; that is why he saves. It also says that he cannot tolerate sin. Remembering these truths, we see Jesus Christ as the only Savior of humanity and his cross as the means by which we are saved. With the apostle Paul, we know nothing but Jesus Christ, and him crucified.

PROCEDURE

Review Quiz

Today's questions are all based on the previous session. Remind the group that from now on, the quizzes will include several questions from earlier sessions (but not sessions from Part One).

1. true
2. false (Jesus is equally God and man)
3. false (We believe that Jesus was "conceived by the Holy Spirit, born of the virgin Mary.")
4. false (Jesus means Savior.)
5. true
6. false (Christ means "anointed one" or Messiah.)
7. true
8. true
9. true
10. true

Video Presentation

Before viewing the video, take a few minutes to prepare students for the topic of Christ's atonement. Try to create an atmosphere of quiet reverence. Dim the lights and have some candles burning. Play some appropriate music. Tell the group that today you're going to be talking about Christ's atoning death for our sins. Consider reading the following selection by Cornelius Plantinga, Jr., from *A Sure Thing*:

> And so on Good Friday, Jesus the Christ groans and suffers through the hours of official torture. He is pinned, probably naked, to a Roman crosspiece. Pontius Pilate's joke in three languages is tacked up over his head. He suffers heat and flies and searing pain. He suffers the sneers of bystanders—the kind of people who like to crack jokes and munch popcorn at an execution. He suffers a terrifying sense of abandonment by God his Father. At one point he recites the words of Psalm 22: "My God, my God, why have you forsaken me? Why are you so far from saving me, so far from the words of my groaning?" The Son of God sacrifices his life for something he wants more: the lives of you and me. It is the strangest event in the history of the universe. But for us it is also the mightiest and most gracious.

Have the group turn in their Bibles to Matthew 27:32-54, taking turns reading the verses. Afterward, tell the class to keep this picture in their minds when we discuss the atonement, the topic of today's session. It must never become something we reduce to a definition or a cold set of facts. The atonement is Calvary. It is nothing less than the Son of God sacrificing himself for us.

Then play the video through to the end.

> **TIP**
> You could move the above activity to a spot later in the session, if you so choose. It's important, we think, to convey —in some way—something of the cost that Christ paid for our sins. Be alert to opportunities in the session to make the atonement something more than a legal transaction by which Christ makes a deal with God so that we can live forever.

OPTION

Re-create the images Pastor Lew used to describe the relationship of the two natures. If practical, pour yourself a cup of coffee, add some cream, and ask the group why this is not a good image for the relationship of the two natures (because they are not merged in an indistinguishable way). Then pick up two forks, hold one in each hand, and ask why this is not a good image of the two natures (neither are they totally separate and distinct). Finally, intertwine the two forks and ask how this does show the relationship between the two natures (separate yet overlapping and connected). Repeating these demonstrations from the video will help your group remember them and understand them.

Ask your students if they think Jesus still has his human nature in heaven today—or did he lay that nature aside when he ascended into heaven? Listen to their responses, then read the remainder of Article 19, which clearly states the answer. Ask your students how it helps us to know that Jesus, though he is in heaven with the Father, is still true God and true man. He is still like us.

TIP

If your students are familiar with the Apostles' Creed, take time to say it together (if they don't know it, read it together and encourage them to memorize this timeless creed). If you have time, you may also want to revisit Philippians 2:5-11, which lends warmth and life to the steps of Christ's humiliation and exaltation. Have students take turns reading the verses.

Video Discussion Guide

1. **How many natures and how many persons does Jesus have? Was Jesus divine part of the time, human at others? Why was it necessary for him for him to be both fully God and fully human?**

   As the paragraph that Pastor Lew quoted from Article 19 states, the human and divine natures of Christ are "united in a single person, with each nature retaining its own distinct properties." Be sure your students understand that Christ was not divine one moment, as when he healed the sick, and human the next, as when he suffered and wept. Rather, as Pastor Lew explains, the two natures intersect in one person.

   Most important is why Jesus had to be fully God and fully human. Jesus had to be human in order to suffer and die for us, in order to take our place on Calvary; he had to be divine in order to survive that suffering and dying. You may want to quote Article 19, which says that Christ had to be "true God in order to conquer death by his power; and true man that he might die for us."

2. **As God-man, Christ was both "humiliated" and "exalted." Use the Apostles' Creed to list the five steps of Christ's humiliation and the four steps of his exaltation.**

   The five steps of Christ's humiliation are (1) his incarnation, (2) his life of suffering, (3) his death, (4) his burial, (5) his descent into hell. The four steps of his exaltation are (1) his resurrection, (2) his ascension, (3) his ruling at God's right hand, (4) his second coming.

3. **Suppose your chemistry grades are slipping. Instead of your usual "B"s, you're getting "C"s and "D"s. You just don't try anymore. One day after class, your teacher asks what's wrong and offers to help you. With a great deal of effort, you pull your grades back up. Your teacher is happy and says that you've atoned for your earlier lack of effort. What does the teacher mean by "atoned"? What does Christ atone for? How? And what do we mean when we say his atonement is "vicarious"?**

   Use the chemistry example to help students understand that to atone for something is to make amends, to set things straight. See if the students can give other examples of atonement. For instance, a basketball player has a terrible game, but his last-second shot wins the game for his team. Sportswriters might say that he atoned for his poor performance with the winning shot.

   Christ atoned—made amends—for our sins. How? By his suffering and death, and by his perfect obedience to God. By this painful process he brings God and us back together again (at-one-ment). He reconciles God and humanity by his atoning death. He puts right what sin has put wrong.

His atonement is vicarious—that is, Jesus stood in our place and suffered and died for us.

4. **What did Jesus do that Adam and Eve couldn't do? What do we mean when we say his perfection is "imputed" to us?**

   Talk about the "covenant of works" God made with our first parents: If they obeyed God, they would live forever; if they disobeyed God, they would die. Adam and Eve gave in to temptation, disobeyed, and died; but Jesus resisted the evil one, lived a perfect life, and transfers or imputes his perfection to us. As a result, God declares us "not guilty" when we stand before him. And though we too have disobeyed God, God sees us as perfect and rewards us with eternal life.

5. **Pastor Lew says, "Jesus suffered for *you*. Jesus died for *you*. Jesus went through hell for *you*." Think about that, then write a short response that expresses your personal reaction to God's incredible way of paying for your sins. If you wish, write your response in the form of a note to God ("Dear God . . .").**

   Invite all students to participate, and be sure to do so yourself. Everyone will have an opportunity to read their comments aloud as a prayer in the closing part of today's session.

OPTION

Remind students of the "L" in TULIP: the atonement is limited to those chosen by God for eternal life.

TIP

Be sure not to make God out to be the "bad guy" in the atonement process. It's easy to picture God only as the stern judge from whose wrath Christ fortunately saves us. God's justice and holiness is real, and sin must be paid for. But remind your students that it is God's love and mercy that provides a way out for sinners—a way that cost God his only Son.

OPTION

Distribute copies of Article 21 of the Belgic Confession (Pastor Lew read part of this article on the video). Read it to the group—it's a moving and warm confession of what Christ's atonement means. It will help students respond to the next question in a more personal and meaningful way.

TIP

Again, we are in the sensitive area of personal response. Recognize that some of your students may have questions about the atonement. Some may even be unmoved by what Christ has done for them. Let them know it's OK to express their honest feelings or to decide not to participate in this activity.

Closing

Invite students to respond to Christ's atonement by reading their statements from the previous activity. The result will likely be at least some statements of praise and thanks to God. Be sure to read your own statement aloud. You may want to end by paraphrasing 2 Corinthians 9:15: "Thank you, God, for your indescribable gift!"

> **OPTION**
>
> For a longer passage, try a responsive reading of Isaiah 53. Or, if you haven't yet read Article 21, take turns reading it now.

> **OPTION**
>
> Instead of the above, have students silently say the "Jesus prayer." Explain that this prayer, also known as the prayer of the heart, consists of these words: "Lord Jesus Christ, have mercy on me." Point out that the prayer is based on the cry of blind Bartimaeus (Matt. 20:29-34). The prayer is a way of deepening our awareness of our need for Christ and expressing our deep faith in Christ, just as Bartimaeus did.
>
> Invite the group to close their eyes and relax. Ask them to repeat (silently) the Jesus prayer, either in their minds or with their lips moving slowly. Give them about a minute to do this. End the time by simply saying "Amen" aloud.

WHAT WE BELIEVE
SESSION 15

The Church (1)

SCRIPTURE

Acts 2:42-47; Hebrews 10:25

BELGIC CONFESSION

Articles 27-29

PURPOSE

Today's video begins two sessions on the church. Pastor Lew begins by defining the church as the people of God coming out of the world to come together. When the church meets, it does the kind of things described in Acts 2:42-47. Article 27 further describes the church as "a holy congregation and gathering of true Christian believers." Pastor Lew then describes the marks of the true church (things people *do* to make sure the church is true): pure teaching/preaching of the Word, correct administration of the sacraments, and the faithful exercise of Christian discipline. The church also has several attributes (things that describe what the true church simply *is*). These attributes include oneness, holiness, and catholicity.

After today's session, your students should be more aware of what a true church is and does. They should be able to define the church as described in Acts 2 and Article 27, and explain the marks and the attributes of the true church.

PERSPECTIVE

In the fifteen hundred years that passed between Christ's ascension and the writing of the Belgic Confession, the external form of the church changed in many ways. Not all of that change was good. A duality developed between the hierarchy (priests, bishops, the pope) or "teaching church" and the laity or "faithful." This duality was foreign to the New Testament and injurious to the spiritual health of the faithful. The papacy came to claim infallibility and what was called "powers of jurisdiction"—the authority to absolve subjects from their loyalty to kings. Corruption and false teachings (for example, that salvation is gained by our own merit as well as Christ's) infiltrated the church.

The generation that preceded the writing of the Belgic Confession challenged these changes and attempted to redefine the church. Luther described the church as a "community of saints," thereby switching saints from some select heavenly group to an earthly body of ordinary believers. Calvin and the "Reformed" reformers emphasized sanctification—that is, the idea that the church is made up of ordinary people who are being made holy. Reflecting that emphasis, the Belgic

Confession defines the church as "a holy congregation and gathering of true Christian believers, awaiting their entire salvation in Jesus Christ being washed by his blood, and sanctified and sealed by the Holy Spirit" (Art. 27).

Article 27 also proclaims the oneness of God's people in both testaments. This contrasts with modern dispensationalism's notion that the church is a parenthesis in the history of salvation and that it has no organic connection with Israel. Dispensationalism denies the unity of the covenant of grace. It leaves the new covenant of Jeremiah (31:31ff.) and the promise to Israel still unfulfilled and separates Jews and Christians, the two seeds of Abraham.

Instead, the New Testament teaches the unity of the covenant of grace—that is, that all believers are children of Abraham. "There is neither Jew nor Greek . . . you are all one in Christ Jesus. If you belong to Christ, then you are Abraham's seed, and heirs according to the promise" (Gal. 3:28-29). In other words, God's covenant of grace applies to the church of all ages.

Finally, Article 27 emphasizes Christ's promise that the "gates of Hades will not overcome" the church (Matt. 16:18), and it proclaims the catholicity of the church. This last point was a matter of great concern to the reformers, who were branded sectarians and schismatics by the hierarchy of the church. Calvin's position on the universality of the church was clear: "There are not many churches, but only one which is spread throughout the world." The wording of the Belgic Confession is similar.

The reformers had spotlighted and were challenging abuses in the church that were threatening to destroy it. Against that background, the Belgic Confession proclaimed the necessity for Christians to join the church of Jesus Christ (Art. 28) and identified the marks of the true church (Art. 29).

Martin Luther was among the first to emphasize "the outward signs that identify the Christian church." He taught that the Word was the primary sign of the true church. From that Word he identified other signs: baptism, the Lord's Supper, the public exercise of the keys of the kingdom, and the office of the ministry of the Word (*On the Council and the Church*). Next he listed public worship, cross-bearing, Christian graces, and fruits of the Spirit—the same point made in Article 29 of the Belgic Confession. In his tract *Against Hanswurst* (1541), Luther said that there have always been two different churches in the world—one true, the other false. The true church is the one, holy, universal Christian church. The church of Rome, Luther claimed, had become the false church because it had strayed from its ancient roots and had become apostate.

Although the Belgic Confession speaks in absolute terms of the "true" and the "false" church, it acknowledges human frailty: "Great weakness remains" in Christians even while the Holy Spirit motivates them to "fight against it."

Members of the church are to have faith, flee from sin, pursue righteousness, love God and their neighbors, walk a straight path, and crucify their old nature. Thus the confession recognizes the reality of indwelling sin and points to our only hope in "the blood, suffering, death, and obedience of the Lord Jesus."

Pastor Lew talks about discipline, one of the marks of the true church, as teaching. This emphasis will help your students see discipline in a positive light. Discipline is an attempt to help our brothers and sisters in the faith. It is the work of the whole body of believers, not just of the elders or ministers.

Be aware that Article 28's emphasis on the duty and obligation of Christians to join with the true church must be understood against its historical background: The church of Rome had the empire on its side; those who joined the reformers in challenging its abuses risked punishment or even death. The confession's admonition to join the true church was directed to those who were hesitant, fearing the possible consequences. Join the true church, urged the confession; promote its unity, submit to its instruction and discipline, take on the yoke of Christ, and serve to edify each other "according to the gifts God has given [you] as members of each other in the same body."

Although we live in a time and place of religious freedom instead of persecution, the confession's call to ally ourselves with the true church is still valid. Now, as then, it is the believer's task to discern what is false from what it true, so that, as members of the community of the saints, we may continue to be made holy.

PROCEDURE

Review Quiz

Answers to this week's multiple choice quiz are as follows:

1. true
2. false (Christ atoned for our sins by his death and perfect obedience.)
3. false (Christ alone atones for our sins.)
4. true
5. false (The at-one-ment of the atonement means that Christ brings God and us together again.)
6. true
7. true
8. false (The two natures are separate but connected, like intertwined forks.)
9. false (Christ had to be human to suffer for our sins; he had to be divine to endure that suffering.)
10. true

Video Presentation

Before playing today's video, ask your students how they would respond to someone who asked if their church was a *true* Christian church, not just a bunch of people getting together on Sunday to be entertained or to feel good about being religious. How does their church show that it's a true church of Christ? Give your students notecards and ask them to jot down two or three signs or evidences that their church is a true church.

> **TIP**
> You can increase participation by having the students do the task in small groups. Give each group a sheet of newsprint and a marker and have someone in the group record its responses.

OPTION

Give each student a Styrofoam cup and a crayon or marker. Explain that for the next two weeks you'll be talking about the church. For openers, you'd like them to express their opinion about the church by sculpting or drawing on the foam cup. In other words they are to do something to the cup that reflects what comes to their minds when they think of the church. Point out that this is a creative exercise; there are no right or wrong answers.

Have the students explain what they did and why. Don't hesitate to participate in this exercise yourself—your students will be interested in seeing what you do!

TIP

These questions may lead your students into something of an evaluation of their congregation. That's good—it's important for teens to say what they think about their church. Even negative expressions are better than indifference! You might be surprised at how important some aspects of congregational life are to teens. Do take care not to let negative comments slide into personal attacks on the pastor or other leaders in the church.

OPTION

Read Article 27 of the Belgic Confession with the class. Ask students to take turns reading a paragraph and summarizing what it says about the church.

Sample some of the things students wrote down. Ask them to watch today's video carefully to see if any of the marks or attributes of the true church that Pastor Lew gives match their own answers.

Video Discussion Guide

1. What is the church? For a picture of the first church formed after Jesus ascended into heaven, read Acts 2:42-47. What went on there that still goes on in your congregation?

Pastor Lew describes the church as the people of God coming out of the world to come together—to worship, to praise, to pray, to be instructed, and so on. Ask your group if this is how they would describe the church. Would they add anything? Would they say it differently?

Then distribute Bibles and have students take turns reading the description of the early church (Acts 2:42-47). Go back through the passage with them and draw some comparisons to your own congregation. Teaching, preaching, fellowship, sharing the sacrament of the Lord's Supper, giving to those in need, meeting together, praising God, and growing in numbers are all actions that characterize most congregations today. Ask which things seem to be unique to the early church (signs and wonders, having everything in common, eating together in homes, being filled with awe).

Continue by asking your students to give you some words that describe the mood or the heart of that early church (joyful, praising, sincere, caring, filled with awe, and so on). Do they feel that these same words describe their own congregation? Why or why not?

2. List the marks that Pastor Lew says describe what people do to make sure their church is a true church. What questions do you have about these marks?

Take time to talk about each mark, inviting student questions as you do so.

- The preaching is pure if it faithfully interprets the Bible and doesn't subtract from or add to its teachings. Jesus Christ must be presented as the only way of salvation. The preaching ought to focus first of all on Christ, rather than on human emotions, concerns, and issues.

- The sacraments should be limited to two (communion and baptism), should be practiced regularly, and should not be presented as a means by which we receive God's saving grace (sacramentalism). Reading the forms a church uses for its sacraments is one way of evaluating a church's belief about communion and baptism.

24   WHAT WE BELIEVE • SESSION 15

- Discipline shows itself in faithful members who care about each other, in good education programs (discipline involves teaching, says Pastor Lew), and in helping those members who wander from the church.
- Evangelism is evident in outreach to unchurched neighbors near and far. Talk with your group about how your church does these things—perhaps by supporting missionaries from the denomination, perhaps by a latch-key program or crib ministry or food pantry, perhaps by offering "seeker-friendly" worship services, perhaps by neighborhood service projects carried out by the youth group, and so on.

3. **Besides simply *not* having the marks mentioned above, how else would you describe what could be called a "false church" or a sect or a cult?**

   Begin by asking the kids to mentions some groups they regard as sects or cults (Jehovah's Witnesses, Mormons, Hare Krishna, New Agers, Satanists, and so on). Then talk about what makes these groups "false churches." Read the description of the false church in Article 29: It gives itself more authority than the Word of God, does not submit to Christ, does not properly practice the sacraments, relies on people more than on Christ, and persecutes the true church. Of course, other characteristics could be added: for example, giving its leader too much power, using some other book in addition to or in place of the Bible, tolerating unbiblical practices or beliefs, denying the Trinity, and so on.

4. **Do you think it's OK to date people who say they believe in God (or at least in some "divine power" who rules the world) but never go to church?**

   This question should stimulate some lively talk, especially if there are teens in your group who have dated or are dating non-Christians. Some of the arguments that may come up include the fact that the person believes in God, or at least claims to. That would seem to nullify a passage like 2 Corinthians 6:14, which warns about being "yoked together with unbelievers." However, such a person's belief in God seems to be of a very general nature and may not include Christ and salvation. In addition, the lack of church-going is a real concern—recall Hebrews 10:25, cited by Pastor Lew on today's video. At least we'd want to know the reasons behind this—it may be a lack of interest or opportunity, or it may simply reflect a bad experience the person had with one particular church.

   Students might also mention that dating doesn't mean marriage (but isn't that the main purpose of dating?) or that they may be able to use the relationship to evangelize, bringing the person to youth-group meetings or to church (maybe—but there are better ways to evangelize).

- Paragraph 1: The church is "a holy congregation and gathering of true Christian believers."
- Paragraph 2: The church "has existed from the beginning of the world and will last until the end."
- Paragraphs 3-4: The church "is preserved by God against the rage of the whole world."
- Paragraph 5: The church "is not confined, bound, or limited to a certain place or certain persons. But it is spread and dispersed throughout the entire world...."

OPTION

Point out that many churches have printed mission and vision statements describing their identity, goals, and key beliefs. If your church has such statements, share them with the group. Do the statements reflect any of the four marks?

OPTION

Listen carefully to what your teens say on both sides of the issue. You want them to come to the conclusion that dating unbelievers is not a wise or biblical choice, but they need to reach this conclusion on their own as much as possible. Resist the temptation to jump in with the "right" answer.

5. **What three "attributes" of the true church does Pastor Lew mention? Can you think of other characteristics that you personally would look for when trying to decide on a new church home?**

An easy way to remember the three additional characteristics or "attributes" that Pastor Lew mentions is to recall this line from the Apostles' Creed: "I believe in . . . the holy, catholic church." The church is one, it is holy, and it is universal.

Invite your group to add other characteristics they would look for when seeking a new church home (as they may well be doing when attending college or moving to a new location after high school). Perhaps their list will include such qualities as friendliness, warmth, openness to change, lay participation in worship, activities for young people, an emphasis on evangelism or meeting people's needs, and so on. Be sure to give your students time to express their personal opinions here.

6. **What are some of the ways God has really blessed your church?**

Make a list of the students' responses and use that list during your closing prayer.

Closing

Use the list above to offer a "guided prayer" in which you read an item from the list, then pause a moment while students silently offer thanks for that item (or simply have students take turns praying aloud for items from the list).

Note: Next week's session on the church would be greatly enhanced by the presence of your pastor and/or an elder and a deacon. No preparation is required for these individuals. They would simply meet with the class and participate in the discussion.

OPTION

If you have time, have students complete this question in small groups, then remain in their small group for the closing prayer, taking turns saying sentence prayers of thanks for the items the group listed.

OPTION

Have students write their own prayers for their church, including its blessings but also its specific needs. Invite them to read their prayers aloud.

The Church (2)

WHAT WE BELIEVE SESSION 16

SCRIPTURE

Ephesians 4:1-6

BELGIC CONFESSION

Articles 27, 30-32

(Today's session draws on parts of these articles but does not quote them directly; you may want to read the articles yourself as background material to help you lead the session.)

PURPOSE

In today's video, Pastor Lew returns to the topic of the church, reminding us first that it is one, holy, and catholic. He then defines the church as invisible and visible, militant and triumphant, organism and institute. Next, he talks about how the church as institute is governed, as we take a quick look at elders and deacons, councils, classes, and synod. The Presbyterian model is similar, proceeding from session to presbytery to regional synod to general assembly.

We then look at the values of the church, described as P-1: proper worship; P-2: preservation of tradition; P-3: propagation of the church; and P-4: people's needs. Churches that emphasize the first two traits tend to place less emphasis on the second two and vice versa, says Pastor Lew. He concludes with a look at megachurches, parachurch organizations, computers and churches, and the use of members' gifts.

After today's session, your students should have a greater awareness of what the church is, what it emphasizes in its programs, how it's run, and some of the challenges it faces. They should be able to define various terms related to the church, analyze their congregation's emphasis, and express their personal opinion of the church.

PERSPECTIVE

Our word *church* derives from the Greek word *ekklesia,* meaning "called out." It refers to all those who are called out of this world by the preaching of the gospel to become the new people of God. These "called out" people belong to Jesus Christ, their Savior and Lord, and they make their calling sure by living as "children of God without fault in a crooked and depraved generation, in which [they] shine like stars in the universe . . . " (Phil. 2:15).

But the word *church* has come to refer to a large number of very different realities—consider these examples:

- "The *church* needs new carpeting."
- "My *church* worships twice on Sunday."
- "Our *church* has missionaries in countries all around the world."
- "People do *church* very differently in China than they do here."

While these are all legitimate uses of the word *church,* the Bible only uses it in one sense—as the people of God redeemed in Jesus Christ. We need to keep that in mind. The church is not first of all a building, a congregation, or a denomination. It's first of all people—people all over the world in every place who believe in Jesus and thereby form his body. They are God's own family.

In that sense the church is truly *one*. All believers, regardless of where or when they live, their ethnic background, their status, or their distinctive beliefs, together make up the one true church. Pray that in this new millennium we will finally learn to live that way!

The Belgic Confession reasserts the ancient confession that this one church is "holy." That doesn't mean it's perfect. Not by a long shot! But it does mean that this church is set apart, dedicated, and wholly devoted to God. That reality needs to become evident more and more in a day and age when most people devote themselves to wealth, advancement, and the pursuit of their own happiness. Those who belong to the church have a different purpose for living than those who don't. They live for their Lord and the task Jesus has given them. That's what distinguishes them from everybody else.

This holy church is also one and the same church throughout the ages and in all locations. It shows amazing riches and diversity of form, culture, and tradition. But at heart it's the same church because everywhere it proclaims the same gospel, administers the same baptism, and is infused with the same Spirit.

We may, of course, make all sorts of distinctions to help us understand how this body of Christ functions in the world. You'll find a number of them highlighted in the session, and they are worthwhile for your students to think about. But we must be very careful not to resort to endless quibbling about these distinctions, and we must be doubly careful never to allow them to cause actual divisions. Jesus' high priestly prayer for us in John 17 clearly placed one overarching petition before our heavenly Father: "that all of them may be one, Father, just as you are in me and I am in you. May they also be in us so that the world may believe that you have sent me" (v. 21).

After exploring a number of helpful distinctions, Pastor Lew elaborates on the various ways in which the church is instituted. The Reformed/Presbyterian form is one of three common ways in which the church is organized:

- *Top-down.* Church leadership is set up in hierarchical fashion, with local churches governed by priests, priests governed by bishops, bishops by archbishops, and archbishops by a pope or a patriarch, who is viewed as the supreme representative of Christ on earth. Church members, committees, and councils do a lot of the work, but these are advisory and operate under the authority of the priest, bishop, or the pope/patriarch. Roman Catholic and Eastern Orthodox churches are examples of top-down leadership.

- *Bottom-up.* Each member in the local church answers first and foremost directly to Jesus. Leaders are democratically chosen by the members to serve the congregation. Congregations may form larger assemblies of churches (often called "conferences") but these are voluntary and advisory in nature. Authority rests with the membership of the local church. This congregationalist approach is adopted by most Protestant churches in the Anabaptist and Pentecostal traditions.

- *Elder-led.* This structure seeks to follow Paul's command to "appoint elders [Greek: *Presbyteroi*] in every town" (Titus 1:5). Congregation members choose elders who form the church council (or session). Together with the deacons and the pastor they rule in Christ's name. While the council/session often consults the membership on important issues, the buck finally stops in the council room. As Pastor Lew explains, denominational structures are also given authority to do important tasks, but the authority of the local church council is original, that of the major assemblies is delegated. Most churches in the Reformed/Presbyterian tradition have adopted this model of church government.

No matter which leadership structure is adopted by your church, it is important to realize that we all stand accountable first and foremost to our Lord. In church every function is a matter of service—to Christ, to each other, and to the world. Church leadership is not a matter of privilege or of status but of serving the body. Whoever you are and whatever your situation and strengths, Christ calls you to use your gifts of talents, time, and treasure to build up the family of God.

PROCEDURE

Review Quiz
1. b
2. c
3. b and e
4. d
5. a
6. d
7. b
8. d
9. c
10. a

TIP

Because students are asked to define quite a few terms in questions 1 and 2 (below), you may want to stop the video after the first set of terms (question 1) and again after the second set (question 2). Review the definitions and give students time to write in anything they missed on the video.

OPTION

You could enhance today's session by inviting your pastor, an elder, and a deacon to attend. Their presence would indicate to your students that their opinions about the church are valued by its leaders. And the leaders could contribute their own insights when discussing the questions.

Video Presentation

Begin today's session by distributing notecards and asking your students to complete these two statements:

- The thing I like best about my church is . . .
- The thing I like least about my church is . . .

Don't share responses at this point, but ask students to hang on to their notecards until later in the session (when you're discussing question 3). Proceed to play the video, asking students to be alert for the terms in question 1 and the four "P"s in question 2.

Video Discussion Guide

1. **Define the following terms related to the church:**

   - **Church invisible:** All true believers united by the Spirit, including those whom we may not see as members of the visible church.

   - **Church visible:** Members of a congregation; those on the rolls of the church; the people you see in a given congregation. Not all members of the visible church are necessarily true believers.

   - **Church militant:** The church fighting Satan, sin, temptation, and so on.

   - **Church triumphant:** People in heaven.

   - **Church as organism:** Believers doing God's will in every area of life; the people of the church doing things outside of the formal structure of the church.

   - **Church as institute:** The official organization of the church, how it does its business, how it is run (elders, deacons, council, session, classis, presbytery, synod, general assembly, and so on). Please substitute the terms your church uses if necessary.

2. **What are the four "P"s that describe the main values of the church?**

   - **P-1:** Proper worship: An emphasis on an effective worship service as a means of pleasing God.

   - **P-2:** Preservation of tradition: An emphasis on the laws, rules, and traditions of the church.

   - **P-3:** Propagation: An emphasis on evangelism and missions.

   - **P-4:** People's needs: An emphasis on helping people in need, both inside and outside the church.

   Congregations that emphasize P-1 and P-2 may do so at the expense of P-3 and P-4, and vice versa, suggests Pastor Lew. Does your class agree with this? For example, does a congregation that emphasizes people's needs and evangelism tend to do less with preserving tradition and proper worship? Does a congregation that emphasizes proper worship and preservation of tradition tend to do less with evangelism and meeting people's needs? Perhaps in today's "blended" congregational worship styles, there's less distinction between the four aspects than there used to be. Still, although all four aspects are present to a certain extent in every church, few are equally active in all four areas.

3. **Which of the four "P"s do you personally think is most important? Which ones does your congregation emphasize? Which ones would you like to see your congregation emphasize more?**

   After two factual questions, the class should appreciate an opportunity to voice their own opinions. Ask students to refer to the notecards they wrote at the beginning of the session. Invite students to read their statements aloud. See if they can relate some of the positive statements to one or more of the "P"s that their congregation emphasizes. In the same way, perhaps some of the negative statements can be related to one or more of the four "P"s that their church could emphasize more.

   > **OPTION**
   > Divide into small groups, share the "like/dislike" statements, then answer the three parts of question 3. Groups could write their responses on newsprint and then share them with the entire class.

4. **Read Ephesians 4:1-6. What do you think this passage has to say to your church? Try making up a slogan or blurb that's based on this Bible passage and that's aimed at your congregation.**

   Let students work in pairs or threes to invent a short slogan that captures the theme of the passage. Certainly a dominant theme is the unity of all believers (though your students may find other themes, such as being loving and patient with each other). Here are some examples:

   - Keep the peace!
   - We are the church—together!
   - We don't have it all together, but together we have it all.
   - "I don't like living in a divided house." God

   Share the slogans with the whole group (if church leaders are present, be sure they participate in the slogan-writing). Consider asking for permission to run the slogans in your church's newsletter or display them on the bulletin board.

   > **OPTION**
   > Have the groups design a poster to go along with slogan. Supply newsprint and markers and other poster-making materials. Display finished posters in your church foyer.

5. **When have you really felt the oneness with other Christians that Ephesians 4:1-6 talks about?**

   Let your teens think about this for a moment, then ask for examples. Perhaps someone sensed the oneness of believers at a communion service or on a service project that the whole congregation participated in. Many teens attend national youth conventions sponsored by their denominations; often they experience a great bond with other kids and with leaders.

   > **TIP**
   > Have your own example ready so that you can "prime the pump" if students have a hard time thinking of their own examples.

6. **Pastor Lew comments on the importance of members using their gifts to serve their Lord and their church. Think about the abilities, gifts, interests, and character traits that God has given you. Then jot down one way you could use (or are using) one or more of your gifts to serve God and your congregation.**

   Be sure students aren't thinking only about mega-gifts and abilities here! You may want to give them some examples to get them thinking. For instance, someone who enjoys drama might volunteer for the church's drama team; someone who likes little kids could volunteer to serve in the nursery; someone who likes to organize could assign jobs for preparing a spaghetti supper; someone who sings or plays an instrument could participate in the music program; someone who likes to draw could help design bulletins for children; someone who is compassionate could serve in the food pantry, and so on.

   Once all students have listed something, encourage them to follow up on their ideas. Just writing them down doesn't do much good!

7. **Remembering our congregation in our prayers is one way we can all serve. List some areas of challenge or concern to pray about.**

   Last time we suggested your group list the ways God blessed your congregation; today we suggest you focus on the needs and challenges facing your congregation. Let the students speak out of their own experiences of church: in worship, in the education program, in the youth program, in service projects, in the choir, and so on. Compile a list on your board or on newsprint that can be used for your closing prayer.

Closing

Invite students to offer sentence prayers for their congregation, using the lists they've compiled. Or, if you prefer, lead the group yourself, reading each item and pausing to let students pray silently for that item.

Encourage your students to continue to pray often for their church. And encourage them to use the gift they've identified in question 6, above.

OPTION

To increase accountability, have students pair off and tell their partners what they wrote for question 6. Partners can set a time to check with each other on their progress in implementing their ideas.

OPTION

Divide into small groups and have each group make its own list. Groups could share their lists with the class to use during the closing prayer, or they could keep their lists and take turns praying for the various items within their own small groups.

OPTION

Have students write their own prayers for the needs of their congregation. Invite them to read their prayers aloud.

WHAT WE BELIEVE
SESSION 17

Sacraments: Baptism

SCRIPTURE
Genesis 17:7, 11-12; Matthew 3:13-17; 28:19; Acts 16:31-34; 22:16; Romans 6:1-4; Galatians 3:29

BELGIC CONFESSION
Article 34

PURPOSE
Pastor Lew begins today's video by quoting Article 34 and explaining how the water of baptism is a symbol of Jesus' blood washing away our sins. He notes that baptism of adults is done in the context of profession of faith. Why then do we in the Reformed/Presbyterian tradition baptize infants? One reason is to remind us of God's covenant promise to Abraham and his descendants to always be our God. In the Old Testament, circumcision of children and new converts was the sign of God's covenant promise; now baptism is the sign. Some Christians, however, argue that only persons who are capable of professing their faith should be baptized—and then not by sprinkling but by immersion. In support of this view they cite biblical examples and the idea of being buried with Christ and raised to new life (Rom. 6:4). Sprinkling, however, is also supported by the Bible. The video concludes with a baptism by immersion of a teenager from Pastor Lew's church.

After today's session, your students should have a better understanding of baptism, especially infant baptism, and the impact it has on their lives. They should be able to explain what the water of baptism represents, tell why the church baptizes infants, describe the opposing Baptist view, and give specific examples of how God is working in their lives to lead them to himself.

Note: Today's video does not explain what sacraments are. That information is given at the end of the next session, after students have looked at the sacraments of baptism and the Lord's Supper.

PERSPECTIVE
The Belgic Confession teaches that the chief significance of baptism is cleansing; that is, baptism signifies the washing away of our sin. The confession also recognizes baptism as a sign of the covenant and of regeneration. Acts 22:16 and Titus 3:5 describe the cleansing aspect of baptism; Acts 9:17-18; 10:45-48; 11:16; 19:1-6; 1 Corinthians 12:13; and 2 Corinthians 1:22 associate baptism with the gift of the Holy Spirit; and these and other texts point to baptism as a sign of the

covenant. Moreover, Colossians 2:11-12 shows that baptism replaces circumcision as the sign of the covenant (Gen. 17:1-7; Rom. 4:11).

A further meaning of baptism is union with Christ. This idea is taught in Romans 6, and some authors see it as the central meaning of the sacrament. If we also include the reminder of our *need* for cleansing as part of the significance of baptism, we see that this Christian rite is rich in meaning.

How did baptism arise in the church? Ceremonial washings and baptisms took place within the covenant community before the inauguration of Christian baptism, and they assumed ever greater spiritual meaning.

"Wash me, and I will be whiter than snow" (Ps. 51:7).

"Wash and make yourselves clean" (Isa. 1:16).

"I will sprinkle clean water on you, and you will be clean" (Ezek. 36:25).

"'On that day a fountain will be opened to the house of David and the inhabitants of Jerusalem, to cleanse them from sin and impurity'" (Zech. 13:1).

Purification with water was practiced with increasing frequency in later Judaism. The Essenes bathed daily for religious reasons. The Pharisees washed ritually before each meal (Luke 11:38). The Sadducees also had "various ceremonial washings" to cleanse priests, animals, and people (Heb. 9:10-11, 13, 19, 21).

In view of such frequent and repeated washings, it is not surprising that acts of purification by water took on a more profound spiritual significance in Jewish religious practice, marking the transition of the person baptized into a new stage of life. The baptisms of John the Baptist, proselyte baptism, and the baptism of Jesus' disciples (John 3:22; 4:1-2) took place before the institution of Christian baptism.

When Jesus instituted Christian baptism, therefore, he was making use of a religious rite well known to the Jewish people. But Christian baptism was unique because of its rich meaning and because it was done in the name of the Father, Son, and Holy Spirit. A careful reading of Article 34 of the Belgic Confession will help you prepare for this class. The article ends by justifying infant baptism on the basis of the covenant of grace. "Baptism does for our children what circumcision did for the Jewish people. That is why Paul calls baptism the 'circumcision of Christ.'"

God's established covenant with Abraham, the father of all believers (Gen. 17:7), is the background against which the history of Israel, the ministry of Christ, and the rise of the church must be understood. Little children were included in that covenant community, and circumcision, the sign of the covenant, was given to them as well as to adults. The "seed of Abraham" is mentioned each time the promise was given or repeated (for example, Gen. 17:10-14).

The Christian church, growing out of Israel, is the covenant community of this age. This was foreseen in the promise to Abraham; all the families of the earth would be blessed through him (Gen. 12:3; Gal. 3:7-9, 13-14, 26-29). Paul uses the figure of an olive tree to illustrate the continuity, or unity, of the old and new covenant. Some of the branches, Jews, were broken off; others, Gentiles, were grafted in. The tree itself, spanning both dispensations, is the continuing community of God's people (Rom. 11:17-24). Jesus said that the kingdom of God would be taken from the Jewish leaders, representing the nation, and would be given to a people who will produce fruit. That group must be the church, which is the covenant community. The promise of the new covenant (Jer. 31:31ff.) and its fulfillment in Christ (Heb. 8; 7:22; 9:15; 12:24; Matt. 26:28; 2 Cor. 3:6), together with Paul's teaching that the dividing wall between Jew and Gentile has been destroyed by Christ, further support the contention that the church, his body, is the Israel of this age.

Little children are members of God's family today as they were under the old form of the covenant. As members of the covenant community, children are entitled to its privileges—one of which is the sign of baptism.

PROCEDURE

Review Quiz

Answers to today's fill-in-the-blank quiz follow; be sure to allow for some variations of the basic answers.

1. invisible
2. triumphant
3. institute or institution
4. militant
5-6. proper worship; preservation of tradition; propagation of the church; people's needs
7-8. pure preaching/teaching; correct use of sacraments; practice of discipline; evangelism
9. atonement
10. Savior

Video Presentation

Before showing today's video, distribute one Bible to each pair of students and give them three to five minutes to find a biblical example of baptism and/or a reference that directly or indirectly supports baptism. If they can't find a specific location or example, perhaps they can give a general description of what they have in mind (i.e., Jesus was baptized). Distribute a couple of concordances, if you have them.

Ask the pairs to report whatever they've managed to find. Perhaps the single strongest command to baptize is found in the Great Commission (Matt. 28:19), a verse you should read with the class. Christ's own baptism is cited in all four gospels (see, for example, Matt. 3:13-17). The baptism of the Philippian jailer and his household is another familiar passage (Acts 16:31-34). And, of course, Genesis 17:7 spells out the covenant promises that baptism confirms.

> **TIP**
> If your students aren't familiar enough with the Bible to do the exercise, simply have them look up and read Matthew 28:19 and perhaps one other passage listed above.

TIP

It may seem obvious, but if some members of your group are new Christians, you will want to be sure they understand that the sacrament of baptism does not remove sin nor guarantee our salvation. Throughout today's session, be careful to include students who have not yet been baptized or who have recently been baptized. You don't want to give them the impression that if they weren't baptized as infants, they are second-class Christians.

OPTION

Read the fourth paragraph of Article 34 of the Belgic Confession to the class. It's an excellent summary of the meaning of the water of baptism.

OPTION

As an alternative to questions 2-5, stage something of a debate between two groups: the first group should defend the view that baptism should be for persons who can profess their faith, and it should be by immersion; the second group should argue that baptism is for infants as well as for older believers, and it should be by sprinkling. Give the teams at least ten minutes to summarize their main arguments on a large sheet of newsprint. Then have spokespersons from the teams present their arguments. After the presentations, the two groups can interact and debate the issue with each other.

Note: There's no need now to read through all the above passages. They'll be cited later in today's session.

Conclude together that the Bible does indeed tell us to baptize. Today's video will help students answer questions often asked about baptism: Why do we baptize infants? Why sprinkle rather than immerse? and so on. Invite them to raise any additional questions of their own at this time. Then play the video through without stopping.

Video Discussion Guide

1. **What does the water in baptism represent? (See Acts 22:16 and Romans 6:1-4.)**

   The symbolism of baptism is especially clear: just as water washes away dirt from our bodies, so the water of baptism represents the blood of Christ that washes our hearts clean from sin (Acts 22:16).

   Especially in the case of baptism by immersion, the water of baptism can also remind us of "being buried" with Christ and rising up again (Rom. 6:1-4).

2. **What is the covenant of grace, and what is its connection to baptism, especially infant baptism (see Genesis 17:7, 11-12; Galatians 3:29)?**

   Reformed/Presbyterian churches believe that the Bible teaches a divine covenant (an agreement God makes with people) that includes families. In the Old Testament, God promised Abraham and his descendents to always be their God (Gen. 17:7). Children were included in that covenant and were circumcised as a sign of their inclusion (Gen. 17:11-12). In the New Testament, the covenant was extended to all believers (Gal. 3:29), and baptism replaced circumcision as a sign of belonging to God and receiving God's covenant promises. Just as children were included in the covenant in the Old Testament, they are surely included in God's covenant family today. Jesus himself said, "Let the little children come to me" (Matt. 19:14).

3. **How does Pastor's Lew's "rich uncle" story help us understand why we baptize infants, even though they don't have a clue about what's going on?**

   Talk about this wonderful little story with your group. It's a great illustration for them to remember. Let your students draw some parallels with baptism; for instance,

   - Just as "rich Uncle Lew" promises to pay for his young relative's college education, so God promises to always be our God. In both cases, it's a wonderful and reliable promise.

   - Just as the golden chain on the child's neck is a sign to remind the parents (and later the child) of the uncle's promise, so the water of baptism reminds the parents (and later the child) of God's promise.

- Just as the child cannot now understand the meaning of the golden chain but someday will, so the baptized infant will someday come to understand the meaning of his baptism. In both cases the promise has great meaning even though the child involved cannot understand it.

- Just as the parents are delighted to receive the uncle's promise, so parents are delighted to receive God's promise. In fact, they promise in return to do all they can to acquaint their child with the meaning of the promise as he grows older.

In summary, our view of baptism is that it is an action of God, not of the person being baptized. God promises to be a God to infants as they grow up. That promise is real and sure even though babies can't understand a word of it. Our response to God's promise comes later, when we are able to understand the significance of our baptism and decide to claim God's promise by professing our faith. This view of baptism differs sharply from the Baptist belief that baptism is something the believer does as a kind of profession of faith.

4. **Christians in the Baptist tradition do not believe in infant baptism. They believe in the immersion of adult believers. Why? (See Romans 6:4; Matthew 3:13-17; Acts 16:31-34.)**

Read these passages with your students and see if they can draw a reason for the Baptist position from each passage. You may also want to ask students to respond to each argument (if they haven't already done so earlier).

- Romans 6:4: Brings out the idea that baptism means union with Christ, being buried with him and raised with him. Clearly, the imagery supports immersion as opposed to sprinkling. And only adult believers have the knowledge and experience to say, "I'm sick of the old life and ready for the new."

- Matthew 3:13-17: Jesus himself was immersed and was baptized as an adult, not a child.

- Acts 16:31-34: The jailer first confesses his faith, then is baptized. Note, however, that not only he but also his entire family or household were baptized, a group that likely included little children.

Students may also comment that the Bible makes no specific mention of children or infants being baptized, while it does mention many adult baptisms. However, this doesn't make the practice of infant baptism unbiblical. In early New Testament times, the emphasis was naturally on the baptism of adult converts, not infants. But just as Scripture offers no definite proof that infants were baptized, neither does it offer any definite proof that they weren't. In fact, the inclusion of infants in families that were baptized—such as that of the Philippian jailer or Cornelius—seems probable.

> **OPTION**
> Now that students have heard arguments on both sides of the issue, pause and ask them if they personally agree with their church's stance or if they think the weight of evidence points toward baptism by immersion. Solicit some opinions and discussion.

5. **What did you learn from the baptism scene on the video?**

Solicit your students' impressions and what they learned from this episode. Were they surprised that a pastor in the Reformed tradition would baptize a

> **TIP**
>
> It takes some courage for teens to talk about their spiritual journeys with their peers. Be warm and inviting, not manipulative. Let them know you're still busy claiming the promises God made to you in your baptism. That process doesn't end with profession of faith.

> **OPTION**
>
> Before participating in this simple but meaningful ritual, explain to your group that in no way are we baptizing or rebaptizing ourselves; rather, we are simply using water as a reminder that Christ's shed blood washes away all of our sins. Proceed by filling a small, decorative bowl with water. Place the bowl on a table or stand in front of the group. Talk briefly about how we are all sinners in need of cleansing; we all need to have the filth of our sin washed away by the blood of Jesus. Comment that the water in the bowl is nothing more than a reminder of Christ's blood that washes away all of our sins. Invite all who wish to acknowledge that they are sinners in need of cleansing to come forward, dip their hand into the water, and touch their forehead, remembering what they are saying by so doing. Afterwards, close with a prayer of thanks for the way Jesus washes us clean and makes us right with God.

young person by this method? They may wonder why the baptism wasn't done in church (because Pastor Lew's church lacks the facilities for baptism by immersion).

One possible idea your students may have derived from this session is that the method of baptism doesn't really matter that much. "As long as the fundamental ideal, namely that of purification, finds expression in the rite, the mode of baptism is quite immaterial," says Louis Berkhof in *Systematic Theology*. Calvinists point out that the Bible itself doesn't insist on immersion. Besides, sprinkling captures the essential meaning of baptism; in fact, as Pastor Lew points out, it is also solidly biblical, suggesting the sprinkling of the Holy Spirit on believer's heads And, of course, it is obviously safer and more convenient for the baptism of infants.

Maybe some of your students also think there's something special about being baptized as teens rather than as infants. Invite comments about this. Be sure they understand that the Reformed tradition does not restrict baptism to infants—persons like Mary (in the video), who came to know the Lord later in life, are also baptized.

6. **If you were baptized as an infant, how has God worked, and how is God presently working in your life to lead you to claim the promises God made in baptism? If you have not yet been baptized, how is God presently working in your life for your salvation?**

The intent of this question is to lead your students—baptized and unbaptized—to reflect on how God is working in their lives to lead them to him. Give them a little time to think, then ask for volunteers to share their thoughts.

Closing

We suggest asking various students to take turns reading the first four paragraphs of Article 34. Then invite them to say a private prayer of thanks for the promises made to them in their baptism and/or for the way God is working in their lives to lead them to him.

WHAT WE BELIEVE
SESSION 18

Sacraments: The Lord's Supper

SCRIPTURE

Matthew 26:17-30; 1 Corinthians 11:23-25

BELGIC CONFESSION

Articles 33 and 35

PURPOSE

Today's video begins with a brief quote from Article 35 that explains the symbolism of the bread and wine in the sacrament of the Lord's Supper. Pastor Lew then talks about the "who" of communion and explains open and closed communion. (*Note: Although it's not discussed on the video, we've added to those an explanation of the term* close communion, *which is a mediating position adopted by some churches, including the Christian Reformed Church.*) To explain the "why" of communion, he talks about remembering, repenting, rededicating, being filled, having fellowship, and the hands of God reaching down to us in love and our hands reaching up to God in response. In talking about the "what" of communion, Pastor Lew defines sacraments as "visible signs and seals" (Art. 33) and then explains that the signs or "pictures" God gives us in the sacraments (the water, the bread and wine) contain something of the meaning of the very things they represent. He concludes by describing covenant-making in the Old Testament, giving us a picture of what Jesus does for us by his atonement.

After today's session, your students should have a better understanding of and appreciation for the sacrament of the Lord's Supper. They should be able to explain the "who", "why," and "what" of the Lord's Supper, defining the following terms: *open, close, and closed communion; four "R"s and two "F"s; two hands;* and how the elements of the Lord's Supper suggest the meaning of the things they represent. They should be able to evaluate the place of the Lord's Supper in their own spiritual journeys.

PERSPECTIVE

In Roman life, the word *sacrament* had a legal meaning. An oath in court or in the army was *sacramentum,* sacred. In a lawsuit, money put in escrow was *sacramentum;* if forfeited, it was used for a "sacred" purpose.

Taken over by the church, the word came to mean something sacred with an inner or hidden meaning. In the Vulgate it was translated as "mystery" (*mysterion* in Greek; Ephesians 1:9; 39; 5:32) and gradually came to be used in the wide sense for any sign with a secret import.

After Augustine's approval of this broad definition of sacrament, prayer, anointing with oil, palms, the sign of the cross, preaching, confirming, visiting the sick, and other rites were called sacraments—along with baptism and the Lord's Supper.

Although some theologians listed as many as thirty sacraments, the church set the number at seven in the thirteenth century. Seven was believed to be a holy number corresponding to the seven deadly sins, the seven virtues, and the union of God (in three persons) and humanity (whose number was said to be four). The church taught that each sacrament corresponded to a fundamental need in life.

The Protestant church joined Luther's attack of the "sacramental system" in his tract *The Babylonian Captivity of the Church.* Luther rejected five rites as sacraments: confirmation, penance, marriage, last rites, and ordination. Protestants recognized only baptism and the Lord's Supper as sacraments instituted by Christ.

But although Protestants agreed on the *number* of sacraments, they often disagreed about their nature. Before long, a controversy between Luther and Zwingli rocked Protestantism. Luther taught the ubiquity of Christ's body, insisting that he is physically present "in, under, and with" the elements. For Zwingli, "eating Christ's body" meant only "trusting with the heart and soul upon the mercy and goodness of God through Christ."

In the midst of this controversy, Calvin articulated a biblically mediated position. Like Luther, Calvin believed that "eating Christ's body" means real communion with and reception of him. Unlike Luther, Calvin said we receive Christ's body and blood not literally, but in a spiritual manner. Moreover, Calvin held with Zwingli that after his ascension, Christ retained a real body of flesh and blood, which is located in heaven. Calvin emphasized that nothing should be taken from Christ's "heavenly glory—as happens when he is brought under the corruptible elements of this world, or bound to any earthly creatures. . . . [Nor should anything] inappropriate to human nature [be] ascribed to his body, as happens when it is said either to be infinite or to be put in a number of places at once" *(Institutes,* IV, xvii, 19).

The Belgic Confession is based on Calvin's position. The sacraments are a pictorial representation, a dramatization of the Word of God, making their appeal to several senses. Calvin says that since we are "corporeal . . . cleaving to carnal subjects," our merciful God condescends to accommodate himself to our capacity, leading us by earthly elements to give us spiritual blessings. The broken bread and fruit of the vine remind us of the broken body and shed blood of Christ; the water of baptism points to our cleansing in him. Article 35 says that in the supper, Christ gives us his "own natural body and . . . his own blood—but the manner in which we eat it is not by the mouth but by the Spirit through faith. In that way, Jesus Christ always remains seated at the right hand of God the Father in heaven—but never refrains from communicating himself to us through faith." This position articulated by Calvin and the Belgic Confession has won wide acceptance within the universal Christian church, even among many contemporary Lutheran and Roman Catholic theologians.

PROCEDURE

Review Quiz

Here are the answers to today's true/false quiz, with false answers corrected.

1. false (It represents cleansing from our sin by Christ's blood.)
2. true
3. false (We believe the Bible teaches us to baptize infants, but it does not do so directly, in so many words.)
4. true
5. false (We baptize people of all ages.)
6. false (We believe that both immersion and sprinkling are biblical.)
7. true
8. true
9. true
10. false (It's called atonement.)

Video Presentation

Before playing today's video, consider reading an account of the last supper from Matthew 26:17-30. Explain to the class that today's session is about the Lord's Supper, and that on the night before he was crucified, Jesus introduced what has become the sacrament of the Lord's Supper.

Read the passage as the students follow along in their Bibles. When you come to the verses describing the breaking of the bread and the pouring out of the wine, you may want to break a small loaf of bread and pour a glass of grape juice, just to add to the realism and mood of the reading.

Play the video through to the end, asking students to jot down definitions of the terms in question 1.

Video Discussion Guide

1. **Definitions**

   - **closed communion:** Only church members may partake of the Lord's Supper.
   - **close communion:** Visitors may partake of the Lord's Supper if they are confessing members of good standing in their home church and if they ask permission from the church leaders. (*Note: As we mentioned earlier, this definition is not included in the video. Be sure to explain its meaning here along with the discussion of open and closed communion.*)
   - **open communion:** All who love Jesus are invited to participate.

> **TIP**
> To help create a mood of quiet reverence, you may want to darken the room and light some candles. If you prefer, you can also move this entire activity to question 1, when you discuss the meaning of "remember."

> **OPTION**
> Ask if the students have any questions about the Lord's Supper, things they'd like to talk about in today's session. If so, jot the questions down and discuss them at appropriate times during today's session.

> **TIP**
> Be sure to explain which policy your church follows. Ask your students to listen for a statement from the pastor at your next communion service that indicates whether it's an open, close, or closed communion.

SESSION 18 • WHAT WE BELIEVE

- **R: Remember.** Ask what we remember when we take communion (that Jesus' body was broken and his blood was shed for us). You may want to have students read the passage Pastor Lew quoted on the video: 1 Corinthians 11:23-25.

- **R: Repent.** Ask why repentance is an important part of the sacrament (because our sins sent Christ to the cross).

- **R: Rededicate.** Ask what we are rededicating (our hearts, ourselves). Why? Because it isn't enough just to say we're sorry for our sins. True repentance means turning away from them and attempting to live the new life of the Spirit. We also rededicate ourselves out of gratitude for the sacrifice Jesus has made for us.

- **F: Filled.** Talk with your group about how taking bread into our bodies for nourishment suggests taking Jesus into our hearts for our spiritual nourishment.

- **F: Fellowship.** We take communion *with* other believers, not by ourselves, to show the bond that we have with each other and with the Lord.

- **two hands:** Ask what God's hands reaching down to us tell us ("I love you. I'm going to put my mark on you in baptism. I'm going to walk with you for the rest of your life."). Ask what our hands reaching up to God say to God ("Lord, I have faith in you. I believe your covenant promise to always be my God."). In other words, in your baptism God reaches down and says to you, "My child." Years later, when you make profession of faith, you reach up to God and say, "My God."

- **sacraments:** Go with a brief definition here. Pastor Lew says sacraments are unique ways the Bible gives us to connect with God and gain a better understanding and appreciation of our faith. The word *sacrament* itself means a sacred or holy act.

2. **Article 33 of the Belgic Confession says that sacraments are "visible signs and seals of something internal and invisible." A sign is a picture, something we can see that gives us a message of some kind; a seal is a kind of guarantee, an assurance that something is true and will work. So how is the Lord's Supper a sign and a seal?**

   The Lord's Supper is a sign in that the broken bread and poured-out wine represent Christ's broken body and shed blood. It is a seal in that it is an assurance or guarantee that Jesus' death was real and resulted in our salvation. Berkhof includes both "sign" and "seal" in his definition of sacraments, as follows: "A sacrament is a holy ordinance instituted by Christ, in which by sensible signs the grace of God in Christ, and the benefits of the covenant of grace, are represented, sealed, and applied to believers, and these, in turn, give expression to their faith and allegiance to God" (*Systematic Theology*).

TIP

Be sure your students understand that we do not believe that the bread and wine actually become the body and blood of Jesus (the Roman Catholic view). See Perspective section for more comments on this.

OPTION

As a summary of this section, you may want to distribute and read paragraph four (Article 35) of the Belgic Confession—the same section that Pastor Lew reads on the video.

TIP

"Signs and seals" is part of our vocabulary of faith, but it's not a phrase that we use in everyday conversation. So be sure your students understand what it means. If they prefer to say "pictures" for signs and "guarantees" for seals, that's fine.

3. **Would it be all right to substitute potato chips and Coke for the bread and wine or grape juice of the Lord's Supper? Why or why not?**

   It would be all right in the sense that the bread and wine are not magical or special; they are merely symbols. But the problem is that the sign and seal are supposed to contain something of the idea or purpose of the thing represented. The bread reminds us of how Jesus, the bread of life, was broken for us. The wine or grape juice reminds us of how Jesus, the vine, poured out his blood for our sins. Jesus himself is represented by the symbols. This would be missing if other food and drink—such as chips and Coke—were used in the sacrament.

4. **What is the covenant of grace? With whom was it made? What did God promise to do? What is our response supposed to be? What does the covenant of grace have to do with the Lord's Supper?**

   The covenant of grace was a covenant made between Abraham (and his descendants) and God. In it God promised to bless Abraham, to bless the nations through him, and to be a God to Abraham and to his children. Today, all who believe in the Lord Jesus are Abraham's children (Gal. 3:29).

   In return for his covenantal love, protection, and blessings, God wants our faith and obedience.

   Jesus' sacrificial death on the cross—which we remember in the Lord's Supper—fulfilled the covenant of grace by providing all believers with salvation.

   So the sacrament reminds us of how God kept his salvation promises made in the covenant of grace.

5. **Why do you think God gives us the sacraments?**

   Let students give all the reasons they can think of. A good answer is that the sacraments make our faith strong. They help us remember God's covenant promises to us. They remind us of what Christ did for us on Calvary. They bring us closer to God and to each other.

6. **Talk about your own experiences in taking communion (or anticipating taking it after you profess your faith). What benefits do you receive or expect to receive? Does the way the sacrament is presented in your congregation help or hinder you?**

   There's a bit of overlap between this question and question 5, but our intent here is to come down to the personal level. Has participating in the Lord's Supper (or anticipating doing so) helped your students draw closer to God and to fellow Christians? If so, how? Also, give your students an opportunity to comment on the way communion is conducted in your church. For example, if your church practices the "intinction" method of communion (in which members come forward, receive the bread from an from an elder, and then dip it into the

---

TIP

This question relates back to the comments that Pastor Lew made in the previous session. It's such a central part of our theology that we feel the review is a good idea.

OPTION

Take this one step further by asking why we need the Bible *and* the sacraments. If you're using the Belgic Confession as part of this course, take time to read Article 33 (today's video quotes just one line), which says that God gave us sacraments because he knew we are weak; without them we would soon forget or begin to doubt God's promises. The sacraments, says Article 33, seal God's promises in us, pledge his good will and grace toward us, and nourish and sustain our faith. They use our external senses (sight and smell and taste and touch) to show us what God does internally, in our hearts.

OPTION

Invite one or more guests to talk about their experiences at the Lord's Supper. An elderly member of the church, whom your students know and respect, could be especially good for your students to hear. So would, say, a college student who can talk about how he or she is blessed by participating in the sacrament while away from home.

> **TIP**
> Be aware that your students may well be at different places when it comes to participating in the Supper. Some may have made a simple and early profession of faith and may have been taking communion for years. Others may have professed their faith much more recently. And still others are not yet ready to do so. Be sure to affirm that the Lord works differently in different people—his timing varies.

> **TIP**
> This question is for the benefit of those who haven't professed their faith. If all your students have already done so, you should probably skip this question.

> **TIP**
> It may be helpful to explain the procedure your congregation follows for profession of faith. Sometimes teens don't profess their faith simply because they don't know what steps to follow or because they have heard intimidating things about answering questions put to them by the elders, and so on.

> **OPTION**
> Divide into two groups, distribute Article 33, and read it responsively.

wine), how do students like that, as opposed to the method of passing the bread and wine down the rows? Are there other elements that make the communion service especially meaningful to them? Are there ways it could be made more meaningful?

7. **How can we know when we are ready to profess our faith and participate in the Lord's Supper? What kinds of questions should we ask ourselves?**

Work with the group to jot down a few key questions based on their own experience. Here are some examples:

- Do I love the Lord Jesus?
- Do I have faith that Jesus died for me and that he cares for me from day to day?
- Do I feel that I'm missing something by not taking part in the sacrament?
- Do I know what communion means? ("discernment")
- Am I ready to show by my life and my words that I love the Lord?

Accept your students' comments about not being ready, but assure them that if they can sense the beginnings of faith, discernment, and witness in themselves, they are ready to profess their faith and come to the Lord's Supper. If they wait until they are perfect or nearly perfect, they will never come.

We hope you have some students in your class who have already professed their faith and have taken communion. If so, invite them to tell about their own decision to become professing members. Ask them to tell how they knew they were ready.

Closing

Ask your students to "pass the peace" to one or two other persons. One person says, "The peace of God be with you"; the other responds, "And also with you."

Dispensationalism

WHAT WE BELIEVE — SESSION 19

SCRIPTURE
Genesis 17:7; Isaiah 52:7-10; Matthew 28:18; Galatians 3:29; Colossians 2:11-12

BELGIC CONFESSION
No specific references in today's session.

PURPOSE
Today's video begins by noting that Christians take a linear, not a circular, view of time. However, some Christians known as dispensationalists divide linear time into seven distinct time periods or dispensations, each characterized by a unique way in which God deals with his people. The seven dispensations are innocence, conscience, government, patriarchs (also called promise), law, grace (the dispensation we're in today), and the kingdom or millennium. Pastor Lew contrasts this view of history with Calvinism's view—that history is of one piece, tied together by the covenant of grace, and that God's Old Testament promises are still valid today. The video concludes by using circumcision and baptism as examples of the unchanging and continuing nature of God's promises—only the outward sign changes. Dispensationalists see no connection between circumcision and baptism because they happened during separate time periods.

After today's session, students should be aware of the consequences of accepting the dispensationalist view of history. They should feel secure in knowing that Christ is in control of the past, present, and future. They should be able to contrast the dispensationalist view of history with the Calvinist view of history, explaining the implications of each view, especially for the sacrament of baptism.

PERSPECTIVE
The Reformed view of the history of redemption as a unified whole challenges the interpretation of Scripture called dispensationalism, a way of dividing history into seven dispensations, in each of which God changes the way he deals with people. Here we pay particular attention to three of these dispensations: promise or patriarchs (from the call of Abraham until Mount Sinai); law (from Sinai until the cross of Christ); and grace (from the cross until the second coming).

Dispensationalism sees no organic connection between Old Testament Israel and the church. It denies that the church is the true Israel and that the kingdom foreseen in the Old Testament is fulfilled in the church. According to notes in the *Scofield Bible,* which promotes the dispensationalist view, the church is a mystery "committed to Paul. In his writings alone we find the doctrine, position, walk, and destiny of the church" (p. 1252).

Dispensationalism creates a sharp distinction between the various time periods and the way in which God deals with humanity in each. In the Old Testament "legal obedience [is] the condition of salvation"; grace "begins with the death and resurrection of Christ." "Law is connected with Moses and work; grace with Christ and faith" (p. 1115). In this way, law and grace are set over against each other in an unbiblical way. Thus the note to the petition "forgive us our debts, as we forgive our debtors," reads: "This is legal ground. Cf. Eph. 4:32, which is grace. Under law, forgiveness is conditioned upon a like spirit in us; under grace we are forgiven for Christ's sake" (p. 1002). Grace is "constantly set in contrast to law" (p. 1115). The Christian is not under the conditional Mosaic Covenant of works, the law, but under the unconditional New Covenant of grace (p. 95).

According to the dispensationalist understanding of the history of salvation, Christ came to sit on David's throne. That was the message John the Baptist preached. It was also what Jesus expected until the Jews rejected him. At that time the kingdom offer was withdrawn. It will be renewed during the days of the Antichrist and will be accomplished during the millennium, the seventh dispensation. Dispensationalists say the fulfillment of Old Testament prophecy will come during the millennium; during the present "church age" there is no fulfillment. H. A. Ironside, pastor of the Moody church in Chicago, put it this way: "The prophetic clock stopped at Calvary. Not one tick has been heard since. From the moment Jesus bowed his head and yielded up his spirit to the Father, all the glories of the kingdom spoken of by the Old Testament seers and prophets have been in abeyance" *(Mysteries of God,* p. 54).

The New Testament view of history is unlike that of dispensationalism. Law and grace are not contrasted (Rom. 3:31; 7:12); there are no radical breaks between dispensations (Gal. 3:6, 29); and there is fulfillment of Old Testament prophecy in the present age: "All the prophets . . . foretold these days" (Acts 3:24).

It is not surprising that dispensationalism, which ruptures the covenant of grace, repudiates infant baptism; it denies that the people of God, including children, are a continuing covenantal community throughout the history of salvation. The Reformed view holds that this continuing community is based on the covenant of grace God made with Abraham, the father of all the faithful. Infants, as part of the covenant community then and now, receive the sign of the covenant. The sign was circumcision (Rom. 4:11); now it is baptism (Titus 3:57). Baptism symbolizes cleansing from sin (Acts 22:16; Rom. 6:4; Titus 3:5); so did circumcision (Col. 2:13). The two rites are so similar in significance that Paul equates them in Colossians 2:11-12. Baptism and circumcision stand for the same covenantal relationship to God during two different periods. Baptism has taken the place of circumcision.

PROCEDURE

Review Quiz

Here are the answers to today's true/false quiz (with false answers corrected):

1. true
2. true
3. true
4. false (They point us to Christ's atoning death.)
5. false (The bread and wine do contain something of the meaning of the death of Christ.)
6. true
7. false (The two "F"s are "fellowship" and "filling".)
8. false (It's not the elder's hands but our hands reaching toward God.)
9. true
10. true

Video Presentation

Before showing today's video, ask students to think of one event from the past—distant or recent—that they would like to have witnessed. See if each person can mention something and briefly tell why that event interests them.

Then point out that over the years the church of Jesus Christ has tried to figure out how past and present events fit into God's master plan. For example, do the same kinds of events just keep happening over and over as the centuries go by?

Is history like a big, endless circle? Or are the events of history more like a straight line moving toward some grand ending? Can history be divided into a number of distinct time periods, each with its own unique characteristics?

Explain that today's video will present two views of history: the dispensationalist view (refer to the term on the session guide) and the Calvinist view. Ask students to be alert for the basic difference between these two views. They need not attempt to fill in the blanks in question 1 as they watch the video—the group can do that together after watching the video.

Video Discussion Guide

Review this section with your students. Answers are written in **bold** type.

1. Dispensationalist churches believe history is divided into **seven** distinct time periods or dispensations. During each time period God **changes** the way in which he deals with his people; he also tests obedience in different ways. There is little or no continuity between time periods.

> **OPTION**
> Stop the video after Pastor Lew describes each dispensation. Fill in the missing words (from question 1) with your class, then return to the video and the next dispensation.

> **TIP**
> Sometimes, in our enthusiasm for what *we* believe as opposed to what *others* believe, we can get a little carried away with what we regard as the superiority of our own view. Throughout today's session, you will have many opportunities to show your students that Christians can disagree over certain issues and do so with respect and good will. Though the differences between Calvinists and dispensationalists are sharply drawn and have far-reaching implications, they should not divide the body of Christ. Our students shouldn't get the impression that we Calvinists have all the right answers and that others are somehow second-rate Christians.

- First dispensation: innocence

    Adam and **Eve** lived in a state of perfection or innocence. God said, "**Obey me and live forever.**" But they disobeyed and death entered the world.

- Second dispensation: conscience

    Sin awakened human conscience. God said, "Follow your moral sense and obey me." A man named **Noah** and his family did exactly that. But the rest of the world did not. As a result, God was forced to **destroy the world with a flood.**

- Third dispensation: human government

    During this time God related to people through authority figures and leaders. But, as indicated by the **tower** of **Babel**, the leaders disobeyed. And so God gave up his plan of world government and confused and scattered the people.

- Fourth dispensation: patriarchs (or promise)

    God called **Abraham** and gave him many great promises. He began a great new nation of God's people called **Israel.** Under the leadership of **Moses**, God's people were led out of slavery. But even great leaders weren't enough to convince them to obey God.

- Fifth dispensation: law

    At Mount **Sinai**, God began a new era of relating to his people Israel through external laws and procedures. But once again God's people didn't listen. They failed to keep God's law, and so they ended up in **captivity** in Babylon, though a remnant returned to Jerusalem. At the end of this dispensation, God sent **Jesus** to fulfill the law, but the people rejected him and killed him.

- Sixth dispensation: grace and the church

    At **Pentecost** the Spirit descended and the Christian **church** began. God relates to his people through their acceptance or rejection of Jesus Christ. This is the dispensation in which we are living; it will end when **Jesus returns.**

- Seventh dispensation: kingdom or millennium

    The final dispensation will be Christ's **thousand**-year reign in Jerusalem on the throne of David. During this time of prosperity and peace, **the Jews** will be given another chance to accept Christ. When this dispensation ends, **eternity** begins.

Pause for a moment after filling in these simple facts to ask if students have any additional questions about the time periods (remember, next week's session will look at the millennium in detail).

TIP

If you would like more information on dispensationalism and related topics, Andrew Kuyvenhoven's *The Day of Christ's Return* (available from CRC Publications) would be a great resource to guide you through the next couple of sessions.

2. **How does the view of Calvinist Christians generally differ from the view of dispensational Christians? For the Calvinist, what holds history together?**

   The basic contrast between the two views is that of seeing history as one piece (the ruler) versus seeing history as fragments (the bricks). For the Calvinist, history is held together by the covenant of grace. The promises God made in that covenant hold for all of history. Take a moment to reinforce this by having students look up the covenant promise in Genesis 17:7 and its extension to all believers in Galatians 3:29.

   > **TIP**
   > Question 2 is intended only to get at the broad differences between the two views. Details of those differences are explored in question 3 and in the next two sessions.

3. **How does the view of dispensational Christians differ from that of Calvinist Christians on the following issues?**

   - **the Bible**

     Dispensationalism tends to divide the Bible into different "time zones," each zone having its own rules about the way God relates to people, each unique, distinct from all others. As the Perspective section explains in more detail, dispensationalism sets law (Old Testament) and grace (New Testament) over against each other; Calvinism sees law and grace as part of the same system. Also, unlike Calvinists, dispensationalists believe there's no fulfillment of Old Testament prophecies in the present dispensation—they believe that must wait until the millennium. From our perspective as Calvinists, this view of the Bible and history fails to do justice to the magnificent unity of God's great purpose in all of history from Eden to Paradise. It fails see in the Bible the one story of God's developing gracious work with our human race.

   - **God**

     Dispensationalists believe that God changes the fundamental way he deals with people throughout history. It's almost as if God is "trying out" different schemes of relating to people—when one doesn't work, God tries something else. Calvinists believe God's dealings with people remains fundamentally the same. From the beginning, God has one great purpose in mind: establishing his kingdom in the world and bringing it to completion.

     Dispensationalists would say that God has two distinct purposes: establishing an earthly kingdom with the Jews and establishing a heavenly kingdom with Christians. These two purposes do not flow into each other. That's why there must be a thousand-year earthly kingdom before the heavenly kingdom can begin.

   - **the church**

     Ask the students to recall (from the video) when Calvinists say the church began (in the garden of Eden) and when dispensationalists say it began (at Pentecost). Dispensationalists see the church as limited to the current dispensation—that the church has no connection with ancient Israel. The promises made to Israel in the Old Testament do not apply to the church today; in fact, the church today is a temporary reality. Calvinists believe that the church today is the new Israel that is on its way to becoming the perfect people of God. You may want to recall again the two passages that clearly show this link: Genesis 17:7 and Galatians 3:29.

- **infant baptism**

Dispensationalists reject infant baptism because they reject the view that infant baptism replaces circumcision. Circumcision, they say, took place in a different dispensation. It has nothing to do with us today. In the dispensation of grace and the church, baptism is for believers only, not for infants. Calvinists, on the other hand, hold that a sign and a seal given in the Old Testament (circumcision) is continued in the New Testament (baptism). You may want to read Colossians 2:11-12 as a reminder of this continuity.

Of course, there are many other differences between the two views. The next two sessions will focus on how dispensationalists and Calvinists view the end times.

> **OPTION**
> Now that you've talked about some of the differences between Calvinists and dispensationalists, ask your students for their reactions. Do they understand why we take the position we do? Do they agree that knowing about the differences is worthwhile and important for us?

> **OPTION**
> If time permits, have students work in small groups to outline a short response to this statement, then report to the class. Invite response to the entire statement, not just the final question.

4. "How can you be optimistic about the future when you look at the past and present? It's pretty obvious, isn't it, that Satan's in control of this world? Any thinking person can see that the world isn't getting any better. War, poverty, racism, violence, starvation, AIDS, greed, terrorism, shootings at schools . . . you name it, we've got it. So you're a Christian—what difference does that make, other than giving you a way out of this mess after you die?"

How would you respond if someone said this to you?

Many responses could be given, but one key idea should be stressed: Satan is not in control of this world, as dispensationalists tend to suggest. God is. He rules the world through Jesus Christ. All history centers in him. What happened before Christ was shaped toward him; what has happened since is shaped from him. He rules it all. Although not all human beings recognize that rule, it is a fact. During these last days between Christ's ascension and his return in glory, our task is to bring in his kingdom in anticipation of when he will bring it in perfectly and finally.

So we view history with confidence. God our heavenly Father controls events—not Satan, not evil men or nations, not blind forces. Jesus, our Lord, reigns, and we are part of his kingdom. What's ahead is not frightening, for it comes from God's hand as part of Christ's kingdom.

As one piece of scriptural evidence of Christ's rule, read Matthew 28:18 to the class. You could also check out the sections from *Our World Belongs to God* that are quoted at the end of this session.

5. **A long time ago, a Reformed statement of faith was written that began with the question "What is your only comfort in life and in death?" A different way of asking that question is, "What is your only hope for the future?" Please think about that, and, if you're willing, share your response with the group.**

   Give students time to think and to write a couple of sentences in response. As with other personal response questions, encourage them to let their statements reflect honestly where they are on their spiritual journeys.

Closing

Ask for volunteers to read the statements they've just written to the group. You want students to leave your classroom knowing that God is in control, that our world is in God's almighty hands. Isaiah 52:7-10 states this memorably. We suggest closing your time together by reading it to the group or asking a student to do so.

OPTION

Our World Belongs to God is a contemporary testimony of the Christian Reformed Church. It has many beautiful sections that affirm God's rule over our world. Here are several that you could duplicate and read with your group:

1. As followers of Jesus Christ
   living in this world—
   which some seek to control,
   but which others view with
       despair—
   we declare with joy and trust:
   Our world belongs to God!

5. God holds this world
   in sovereign love.
   He kept his promise,
   sending Jesus into the world.
   He poured out his Spirit
   and broadcast the news
   that sinners who repent and
       believe in Jesus
   can live
   and breathe
   and move again
   as members of the family of God.

13. God directs and bends to his will
    all that happens in his world.
    As history unfolds in ways we only
        know in part,
    all things—
    from crops to grades,
    from jobs to laws—
    are under his control.
    God is present in our world
    by his Word and Spirit.
    The faithfulness
    of our great Provider
    gives sense to our days
    and hope to our years.
    The future is secure,
    for our world belongs to God.

WHAT WE BELIEVE
SESSION 20

End Times: Premillennialism

SCRIPTURE
Matthew 24:4-8, 22, 30-31, 36, 40-42; 1 Thessalonians 4:13-18; Revelation 13:16-18; 20:1-4, 7-10, 11-13

BELGIC CONFESSION
No specific references in today's session.

PURPOSE
Today's video explains the dispensationalist (especially the premillennial rapturist) view of the end times. First, a trumpet will sound and the rapture will take all believers, dead and alive, to meet Christ in the sky. Seven years of tribulation on earth will follow, during which unbelievers will receive the mark of the beast. Then Christ will publicly return with all the believers. Satan will be bound in a pit, and Christ will reign triumphantly from Jerusalem for a thousand years of prosperity and bliss. Near the end of the thousand years, Satan will emerge and wage a brief but bloody war against Jesus and his followers, but Christ will destroy him. Then God will judge his people. Over against this view, Calvinists recognize only the second coming of Christ and the final judgment (next week's session will focus on the Calvinist position).

After today's session, students should have a heightened awareness of the end times. They should be able to explain the premillennial rapturist view of the end times, identifying terms such as *the rapture, tribulation, the mark of the beast, millennium,* and *judgment.* They should be able to briefly state the Calvinist position on the end times and describe their own attitude toward the coming judgment.

PERSPECTIVE
The word *millennium* comes from the Latin word for one thousand. It refers to the teaching in Revelation 20 that Christ will reign and that Satan will be bound for one thousand years. Throughout the history of the church this passage has been variously interpreted. Some take it literally, others symbolically.

In the last century, millennial teaching was articulated by J. N. Darby in England and his American popularizer, C. I. Scofield. Darby held that (1) the church is limited to believers between the first and second comings of Christ; (2) the Old Testament saints were not a part of the church; (3) Old Testament prophecy is directed to the nation of Israel; (4) Christ came to be the king of the Jews. When they rejected him, he withdrew his offer. But during the millennium that offer will be renewed and accepted.

According to Dr. A. Pieters, "Those who hold this 'postponed kingdom' theory deny that Christ set up any kingdom at all at his first coming." The present age is only a parenthesis in the history of salvation, during which no Old Testament prophecy is being fulfilled. As Pieters says, Darby's theory boosted millennarian teaching, for Old Testament prophecy envisions a glorious messianic age with Israel in the center of it. Before Darby, the church believed that prophecy began to be fulfilled with the coming of Christ and that the Christian church, Christ's body, is the seed of Abraham, the people of God, the Israel of this age. After Darby, earlier millennarianism became popularly associated with dispensationalism.

The general features of millennial teaching are these: Christ will establish an earthly kingdom in Jerusalem and reign as king for a thousand years; all functions of government will be under his supervision, and his rule will extend to all nations. Israel will be reconstituted as a nation, animal sacrifices will be reinstituted, and the law of Moses will be the law of the land. Satan will be bound so that he cannot deceive the nations, war and false religions will cease, the curse will be removed from nature, and there will be great prosperity over all the earth. Much of this description of the millennial age comes from the visions of Old Testament prophets—visions that still await fulfillment, according to millennarian thinking. The Davidic covenant assumes great importance (2 Sam. 7:8-16; Ps. 89:3-4, 20-21, 28-37); it "has not been abrogated (Ps. 89:33-37), but is yet to be fulfilled (Acts 15:14-17)" (*The Scofield Reference Bible,* p. 977).

Reformed/Presbyterian churches reject the postponed kingdom theory and the notion that the church is a parenthesis in the history of salvation, having no continuity with Old Testament Israel. The reconstruction of Israel as a nation under Christ as king in Jerusalem and the literal interpretation of Old Testament prophecy as fulfilled in the millennium is dubious at best since Revelation 20 is silent about those prophecies. Premillennialists connect Old Testament prophecy with the millennium by passing this present age of the church. The prophecies, then, have nothing to do with us. In fact, the New Testament says that in Christ the old distinctions are done away; Gentiles are heirs together with Israel, members together of one body (Eph. 3:6; 2:11-22).

Another objection to this theory is its literal understanding of the thousand years. The book of Revelation uses pictures and symbols to state truth. Interpreting the thousand years literally violates sound rules of interpretation. The millennium is better understood as the period between the first and second comings of Christ. At his first coming Satan was defeated and redemption was accomplished. Christ now reigns as Lord. His ministry was a victory over the powers of darkness: when he was an infant, Herod could not kill him; in his temptations, Satan could not make him yield. His ministry set captives free (Isa. 61:1; Luke 4:16-20). After the successful mission of his seventy disciples, Jesus "saw Satan fall like lightning from heaven" (Luke 10:18). And just before his passion, Jesus said, "Now is the time for judgment on this world; now the prince of this world will be driven out. But I, when I am lifted up from the earth, will draw all . . . unto myself." John then says that Jesus "said this to show the kind of death he was going to die" (John 12:31-33). When Jesus was "lifted up," he "disarmed the powers and authorities . . . triumphing over them by the cross" (Col. 2:15).

According to the epistle to the Hebrews, "Since the children have flesh and blood, he too shared in their humanity so that by his death he might destroy him who holds the power of death—that is, the devil—and free those who all their lives were held in slavery by their fear of death" (2:14-15). The gospel message is clear: Christ's victory was complete. As Calvin put it, the devil, though still active, has been bound and has to drag his chains with him wherever he goes.

PROCEDURE

Review Quiz

1. seven
2. grace and the church
3. Christ returns
4. law
5. circumcision
6. one piece, or unified, or like a ruler
7. change
8. remembrance
9. all believers
10. seals

Video Presentation

Explain briefly that Pastor Lew will give details about the end times according to the premillennialists, who hold that Christ's return will precede and bring about his thousand-year reign of prosperity and peace on the earth. Premillennialists belong to the broader group of dispensationalists, who believe that history is divided into seven time periods (see session guide from session 19).

Ask everyone to listen carefully to Pastor Lew's description of the various stages of the end times. They should pay full attention to the video and not try to jot down notes this time (you'll be going back through the various stages together after the video). Tell the class that today's session will focus mainly on the premillennialist view of the end times; next week's session will present the Calvinist view in detail.

Video Discussion Guide

1. What support does Revelation 20:1-3 give for the millennium or dispensation of one thousand years? What do *pre*millennialists believe?

The verses from Revelation that Pastor Lew quotes are about Satan being bound for one thousand years. If we take this literally (which Reformed churches do not), then it would indeed support the block of time called the millennium.

> **OPTION**
> To get students into the "future" mode of the next two sessions, begin by asking for a show of hands from those who think Christ will probably return during their lifetime. Next, ask for a show of hands from those who feel that he probably won't return during their lifetime. Finally, poll those who have no strong feelings either way. Talk a little about the reasons behind their responses; then comment that the next two sessions will focus on the return of Christ.

> **OPTION**
> Stop the video after Pastor Lew's explanation of the rapture, of the tribulation, and so on, to give students time to jot notes, look up Scripture passages, and ask questions.

> **TIP**
>
> Giving some examples of local churches (or television evangelists) that hold to a dispensational/premillennial view will help students realize that these ideas are held by many Christian churches today.

> **TIP**
>
> If students are interested in a further description of the rapture, read the following description from John Hagee's *Beginning of the End,* pp. 104-105, as quoted by Andrew Kuyvenhoven in *The Day of Christ's Return:*
>
> All over the earth the graves of those who have trusted Christ will explode as their occupants soar into the heavens to meet the Light of the world.... Cars will empty beside the interstate, their engines running, their drivers and occupants strangely missing. Supper dishes will steam in the homes of believers, food will boil on their stoves, but no one will remain to eat this earthly dinner, for all believers will be taking their places at the heavenly table for the marriage feast of the lamb. The next day, headlines of local, national and international newspapers will scream, "MILLIONS MISSING WITH NO EXPLANATION." New Age devotees might explain the mass disappearance by insisting that a vast armada of UFOs have abducted millions of people.... Telephone lines around the world will jam as families try to check on loved ones. And the churches of the world will be packed with weeping, hysterical people who see the truth too late and cry, "The Lord of Glory has come and we are left behind to go through the Tribulation and to face the coming Antichrist."

Those who are *pre*millennialists believe that Christ's coming will precede and bring about his thousand-year reign on earth.

2. **Fill in details of each of the following events that many dispensationalists and premillennialists believe will happen during the final dispensation (the millennium or thousand years). The passages listed are those often given in support of this view.**

Walk your students through the events and the accompanying Scripture passages. Have them jot down brief descriptions of what will happen. Guidelines follow:

- **The trumpet and the rapture (1 Thessalonians 4:13-18)**

  A loud trumpet will announce the return of Christ; believers, dead and alive, will rise from the earth to meet him in the air.

  According to the *NIV Study Bible,* this is the only passage in the Bible that clearly refers to a "rapture" (being "caught up"). But note that unlike the "secret rapture" described by some premillennialists, Paul seems to be talking about a public event accompanied by loud voices and a trumpet blast. You may also want to read Matthew 24:40-41, verses that are sometimes cited to show the suddenness and the selectiveness of the rapture.

- **The tribulation and the mark of the beast (Matthew 24:4-8, 22; Revelation 13:16-18)**

  During this seven-year period of worldwide war and destruction, a worldwide government called "the beast" will take over. Unbelievers will receive a mark of the beast—some configuration of the numbers 666 (see Rev. 13:16-18) that will allow them to buy and sell. Those who convert to Christ and refuse the mark will be beheaded, but they will go to be with Jesus and the other believers. Although the video doesn't mention it, the Antichrist will dominate the world during this time. Some 144,000 Jews will be converted and will work to evangelize an evil world.

  Note that those, dead and alive, who confessed Christ before his return will be spared all this trouble. Reacting to this, Andrew Kuyvenhoven writes, "Suffering, or tribulation, is part of the Christian life. It is not incidental, but belongs to the way of salvation.... We have much more reason to believe that something strange is going on when the church has peace than when it is under fire" (*The Day of Christ's Return,* p. 76).

- **The millennium**

  a. **Jesus' public return with believers (Matthew 24:30-31)**

     After the seven years of tribulation, Christ will return. Unlike the return of Christ at the rapture, this return will be public and will be witnessed by all people everywhere. It will occur just at the time when it seems the world will destroy itself. Calvinists typically regard the event described in Matthew 24:30-31 as the one, public return of Christ.

b. **Satan locked in the pit (Revelation 20:1-3)**

Note that Revelation 20 will be discussed again next time. You needn't do much with it today, except perhaps to comment that Calvinists don't take the thousand-year binding of Satan literally. Instead they regard it as "picture language" showing that throughout all of history Satan is bound by the power of Christ.

c. **Christ's glorious reign of a thousand years begins (Revelation 20:1-4)**

Christ will rule the nations from the city of Jerusalem for a thousand years of peace and prosperity. The following detail is not mentioned on today's video: Reigning with Christ will be two groups—the believers who returned to earth with him and Jewish people who once rejected Jesus. The Jews will be exalted over the Gentile believers.

- **Satan briefly unleashed, destroyed by Christ (Revelation 20:7-10)**

Toward the end of the thousand years of bliss and prosperity, God will allow Satan to emerge from the pit and make war against Jesus and his followers. After the final battle, Satan will be cast into the bottomless pit and remain there forever.

- **Final judgment (Revelation 20:11-13)**

All unbelievers will now be raised from the dead (believers have already been raised) and God will judge everyone from his great white throne. Those who lived godless lives will be put finally and forever into hell; those who believed and who ruled with Christ during the millennium will live forever and ever in the new earth.

3. **Many Christians today—including many of those who teach "believer's baptism by immersion" hold to some version of the above "end time events." What is your personal reaction to the premillennialist view? What seems reasonable to you? What do you wonder about?**

You shouldn't go into detail here, analyzing each Scripture passage, and so forth. Rather, simply let your students ask their questions and give their reactions. This would be a good time to remind students that people's stand on this issue does not determine their eternal salvation. As Pastor Lew says on today's video, "If I'm wrong and I'm going up in the air and I see the tribulation started, I'll be the first one to turn to my Baptist brother and say, 'You were right!'"

4. **Next week's session will look in detail at the Calvinist view of the end times (especially Revelation 20). For now, just indicate very briefly what Calvinists think will happen at the end of time.**

As we learned last session, Calvinists see history as one piece, not as separate dispensations. They believe there will be just one return of Christ, followed by the resurrection and final judgment.

> **OPTION**
>
> Premillennialists sometimes cite Isaiah 35 to describe the millennium. Read a few verses of that chapter with your group.

> **OPTION**
>
> As you discuss each of the above events and their supporting passages, make a large timeline, using a long piece of shelf paper or several sheets of paper taped together. As you talk about each event, add it to the timeline. A finished timeline would look something like this:

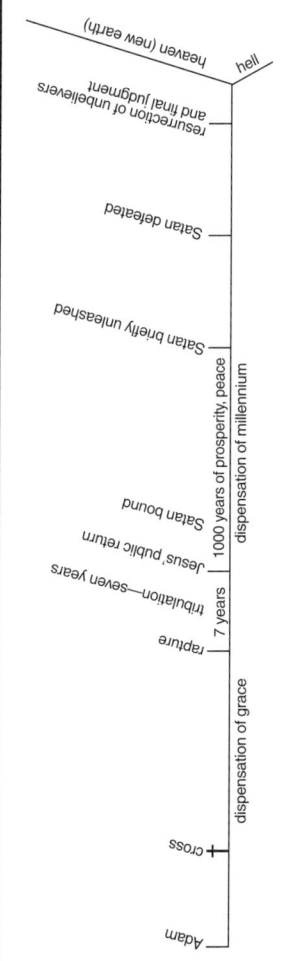

5. **Suppose you knew that Jesus would return in exactly one year. How might you change your life?**

   Invite responses, then comment that the question is purely speculative since no one will ever have this information, despite the rash of predictions of the time of Christ's return (Matt. 24:36). Note verse 42 of the same passage: "Therefore keep watch, because you do no know on what day your Lord will come." Ask students what they think it means to "keep watch."

Closing

Allow a moment of silence for students to look back at their response to question 5. Then invite them to silently ask God to help make just one change in their lives that reflects their awareness of his return in glory someday.

> **OPTION**
> Read Romans 8:1 in unison: "There is now no condemnation for those who are in Christ Jesus." Then say together as your closing prayer, "Thanks be to God for his indescribable gift!" (2 Cor. 9:15).

End Times: The Reformed View

SCRIPTURE
1 Thessalonians 4:13-18; 2 Peter 3:10-13; Selections from Revelations 20 and 21

BELGIC CONFESSION
Article 37

PURPOSE
After reviewing the premillennialist version of "end time" events, Pastor Lew reads a description of the end times from Article 37 of the Belgic Confession, again noting that we are not discussing "salvation issues." According to the Reformed view, the end times will begin with a trumpet blast that announces the return of Christ, which everyone will see. Believers will then be removed from the world (1 Thess. 4:15-18), which will then be burned with fire (2 Pet. 3:10-13). Judgment will follow—unbelievers will be punished eternally, but believers will begin life on a new, refreshed earth (Rev. 20-21). The video ends by asking, "What about those thousand years described in Revelation 20?" The Reformed answer is that Revelation is a book of "pictures" or symbols; the number "one thousand" should not be taken literally but symbolically, as a sign of wholeness or completion.

After today's session, students will have a better understanding of the Reformed view of the end times. They should be able to contrast the Calvinist and premillennialist view, explain why most Calvinists reject the premillennialist view, and how Calvinists interpret Revelation 20. Finally, they should be able to give a biblical picture of the new heaven and new earth.

PERSPECTIVE
A Christian understanding of history says that history is going somewhere. God created a world with time and space. Human history is not "a tale told by an idiot, full of sound and fury, signifying nothing" (Shakespeare, *Macbeth*). By contrast, Christians believe that human history had a beginning, it has direction, and it will have an end.

History has meaning and purpose because it has a Lord who knows every deed (Rom. 2:6) and hears "every careless word" (Matt. 12:36). These human words and deeds will be a part of the settlement when history is complete. "For we must all appear before the judgment seat of Christ, that each one may receive what is due him for the things done while in the body, whether good or bad" (2 Cor. 5:10). Christians believe that the universe is fundamentally moral and spiritual because God, who is the Lord of all, loves righteousness and hates iniquity. The Lord our

God is holy; that is his nature, and that is why all of our life and all of history is so important and why this last article of the Belgic Confession is so important. Everything else that has been said—about the fall, redemption, the church—is preparation for the life to come.

The New Testament teaches that before Christ's return (1) "the full number of the Gentiles" must come into the church (Rom. 11:25); (2) Israel will turn to the Lord (Rom. 11:26); (3) the gospel must be preached "in the whole world as a testimony to all nations" (Matt. 24:14); and (4) apostasy and the Antichrist will appear (2 Thess. 2; Matt. 24:9-12). The grand climax of history, the consummation of God's plan of the ages, will occur "when the time appointed by the Lord is come . . . and the number of the elect is complete" (Art. 37). Then all will see that the three supreme events in world history are the fall by the first Adam, redemption by the second Adam, and the consummation of all things by him.

Article 37 sets before us the second coming of Christ, the purpose of his coming, and its consequences. He "will come from heaven bodily and visibly, as he ascended." "Every eye will see him, even those who pierced him; and all the peoples of the earth will mourn because of him" (Rev. 1:7). His first coming was obscure and humble; the second will be "with great glory and majesty." The first was known to but a few; the second will be seen by all.

The purpose of Christ's coming is to "judge the living and the dead" and to "burn this old world, in fire and flame, in order to cleanse it" (Art. 37). Sin has ruined God's magnificent world and made human history a tale of woe. God will not allow this to go on forever. He will bring down the curtain on the drama of human history, a history of which he has become a part. There will be a reckoning; those made in his image will be called to give an account. This is the plain teaching of Scripture (for example, see Matt. 25:33-46).

Most people feel instinctively that a final judgment has to happen. Even non-Christians who are serious thinkers, people like Immanuel Kant, have argued the necessity of a final judgment in order for humanity to live rationally and morally. For without morality and a final judgment, as a poet has said, "the pillared firmament is rottenness and earth's base stubble."

Besides judgment, Christ's coming will bring restoration. He "must remain in heaven until the time comes for God to restore everything, as he promised long ago through his holy prophets" (Acts 3:21). Creation, "subjected to frustration . . . will be liberated from its bondage to decay and brought into the glorious freedom of the children of God" (Rom. 8:20-21). Then will come the new heaven and the new earth of which the seer spoke, for the first heaven and the first earth shall pass away (Rev. 21:1).

The standard by which God will judge humanity is the distinction, grounded in God's holiness, between right and wrong. There *is* a difference, despite the contrary opinion of some today. That distinction is presupposed in the confession where it says simply that people will be judged "according to the things they did in the world, whether good or evil. Indeed, all people will give account of all the idle words they have spoken, which the world regards as only playing games. And then the secrets and hypocrisies of men will be publicly uncovered in the sight of all (Art. 37). On that day, no one will challenge God, for all will know that his judgments are "sure and altogether righteous" (Ps. 19:9).

The consequence of judgment is the separation of "wicked and evil people" from "the righteous and elect." There will be no group in between. People are either in Christ or outside of him. Jesus told people in his day that there was sufficient witness to him, "yet you refuse to come to me to have life" (John 5:40). That is still true today. In *The Great Divorce,* C. S. Lewis said that there are some who despise the gospel invitation; if they have to choose, they would rather reign in hell than serve in heaven. He also observed that there are two kinds of people in the world: those who say to God, "Thy will be done," and those to whom God someday will say, "Thy will be done." This absolute separation between faith and unbelief is clearly taught in Scripture. In their study of the end times, your students are again challenged to choose the life that is in Christ.

PROCEDURE

Review Quiz

It's especially important for today's session that students understand the sequence of the premillennial timeline. Some of your students are likely to have difficulty remembering the proper sequence of events, so take your time and be sure everyone has the correct information before viewing today's video. The correct sequence follows:

1. sound of trumpet
2. the rapture of all believers to be with Christ in the air
3. the seven years of tribulation and the mark of the beast
4. Jesus' public return with believers begins the millennium
5. Satan locked in the pit
6. the thousand-year reign of Christ (millennium) from Jerusalem
7. Satan briefly unleashed but defeated
8. final judgment

True/false statements:

9. false (They say we are living in the dispensation of grace, or the church.)
10. true

Video Presentation

Explain to the class that today's video is basically an extension of last week's presentation. Then play the video without stopping. Students should simply listen carefully—there's no need now to fill in the blanks of question 1.

> **OPTION**
>
> If you made the optional timeline during the last session, use it again today to help students recall the sequence of end-time events according to the premillennialists.

> **OPTION**
>
> Get the group thinking about heaven by asking them to list three things about heaven that they look forward to the most. It's OK if students want to have some fun with this ("No more homework! Sleeping in every day!") but serious comments are welcome too. Invite students to read their lists aloud. Then comment that today's session will give us, among other things, a look at what the Bible says about the place Christ has prepared for all believers.

> **TIP**
>
> You'll notice that we've added some details not mentioned on the video but implicit in the passages Pastor Lew cited. Should you want more background for yourself, check out chapters 5-7 of Andrew Kuyvenhoven's *The Day of Christ's Return* (CRC Publications).

> **OPTION**
>
> Challenge groups who are more familiar with the Bible to come up with their own sequence of end-time events from the Reformed perspective. Give them the passages above and copies of Article 37. Have them work in groups of two or three to jot down these events on large sheets of paper.

> **OPTION**
>
> It won't hurt to remind students once again that while we believe the Reformed view of the end times is biblically accurate and that of the premillennialists is not, our differences are not salvation issues. Why talk at all about the differences? Let your students suggest their own reasons—they've already heard a couple from Pastor Lew.

Video Discussion Guide

1. **Get the picture of the Reformed view of the end times by filling in the missing words in each event described below:**

   Distribute Bibles for this activity. We suggest you have students work in pairs to complete the exercise. The correct answers are in **bold** type.

   - A loud **command**, the voice of an **archangel**, and a **trumpet** call of God will announce the return of Christ (1 Thessalonians 4:16). **Everyone** on earth will see him coming!

   - The **dead** will be raised first. Then those who are still **alive** on the earth will be instantly changed to immortal beings and will meet **Christ** in the air (1 Thessalonians 4:16-17).

   - Then God will **burn** this old world (2 Peter 3:10).

   - The earth will then be **renewed; refreshed; made new** (2 Peter 3:13; Revelation 21:1). *Note that the word "heaven" here does not refer to the dwelling of God but to the sky and space around and above the earth.*

   - Christ will **judge** the living and the dead (Revelation 20:12). Those who have rejected Jesus will **be punished eternally** (v. 15) but those who love Jesus will live with him forever in the beautiful **new earth** (21:1-3).

2. **How does the Reformed view of the end times differ from the premillennialist view?**

   Differences include the following:

   - The Reformed view holds to only one return of Christ that everyone will witness; the premillennialist view seems to have two: first a "secret" return to remove all believers from earth, then a public return to launch the millennium.

   - The Reformed view does not include a "rapture" that secretly removes believers from a world about to be plunged into seven years of suffering; rather, Calvinists believe that followers of Christ who are still alive when Jesus returns will go instantly to be with him forever (yes, this could be called a "rapture" or "being caught up"). In his book *The Day of Christ's Return*, Andrew Kuyvenhoven says that "perhaps the most objectionable feature of the rapture teaching is the world flight by the church. When the real trouble begins (the great tribulation) the true Christians sail through the sky to the wedding banquet in heaven. With thinly disguised glee, evangelical preachers and authors keep making up stories about the mess the saints leave behind when they fly to the Lord. [But] there is not a hint in the Scriptures that the saints will silently slip out of this world" (pp. 65-66).

   - The Reformed view does not take literally the one thousand years, the tribulation, or the leashing and unleashing of Satan, all of which are part of the premillennialist view.

3. **Suppose that we die before Jesus comes. What happens next?**

   We believe that when we die, we go to be with Jesus. The traditional Reformed view expressed by Calvin, the Belgic Confession (Art. 37), and the Heidelberg Catechism (Q&A 57) is that our souls or spirits are consciously in the presence of Christ immediately after death. Our bodies are, of course, buried, cremated, or otherwise disposed of.

   When Christ returns in glory, we are immediately resurrected and reunited with our souls to full bodily life (Art. 37 and Q&A 57 say that our souls or spirits are reunited with our bodies). Then we and all people—including those still living on earth who met Christ in the air—are judged. Finally, as sinners redeemed by Christ we live with him in the renewed earth.

4. **When you think about the final judgment, which all Christians agree is coming, what are your feelings? Do you tend to see it as a time of celebration, as Pastor Lew suggests, or as a scary time of having to give a public accounting of all your sins?**

   Nobody should be casual about the last judgment. But neither need we fear it, even though we don't know the details of exactly what will happen and how. What we do know, as Pastor Lew says, is that we are forgiven people. All of our sins are covered by the blood of Christ. God has forgiven them and forgotten them. Even the stern warnings in Article 37 about "giving account" are followed by this: "But it [the judgment] is very pleasant and a great comfort to the righteous and elect, since their total redemption will then be accomplished." That sounds a lot like the celebrating that Pastor Lew talks about on the video.

5. **How do Calvinists generally interpret the thousand years, the binding of Satan, and the other events mentioned in Revelation 20:10?**

   As Pastor Lew explains, Revelation is an account of John's vision, a book of pictures or symbols, much of which should not be interpreted literally. The thousand years, for example, could be a symbol of wholeness and completeness, indicating that throughout the time between the Lord's first and second coming Satan will be bound by the power of Christ.

6. **Read Revelation 21:1-5, 22-27. What do you think living in the new heaven and new earth will be like? What will not be present there? What will be present?**

   Missing will be

   - the sea (in Bible times the sea was associated with danger and chaos).
   - tears, death, mourning, crying, pain.
   - the temple (no "going to church" because God is the temple and we will be worshiping God everywhere).
   - the sun and moon (because the glory of God is light enough).

> **TIP**
>
> In 1 Thessalonians 4:18, Paul says that believers ought to be encouraged by knowing what will happen when they die or when the Lord returns. That's the whole point here. Some of your group may have already wept by the grave of a beloved grandparent or parent or sibling. Even if they haven't, they still need to know that when they (or one of their loved ones) die, they go to be with our Lord.

> **OPTION**
>
> Article 37 is a long and rather vivid description of the last judgment. On the one hand, it does say that "all people will give account of all the idle words they have spoken . . . and the secrets and hypocrisies of men will be publicly uncovered in the sight of all." On the other hand, the same article says that the Son of God will confess our names before God his Father. In the final judgment God will clear up with every believer all that might still cause distance between them. Such an accounting will allow believers to experience relief and comfort, and they will stand in awe of God's grace and mercy.

> **TIP**
>
> Have half the class list things that Revelation 21 says will be missing from our new life; the other half list things that will be present.

> **OPTION**
>
> Share with your students some of Cornelius Plantinga's insights from *A Sure Thing*, p. 269:
>
> We usually think of heaven as way up. We think of spirits with airy bodies floating about on cumulus clouds. These pictures must come down. For in Revelation 21 John suggests that the new heaven and new earth will be right here where we now live. Heaven descends to earth, this earth. This earth will be purified and renewed so that heaven can be on-site where we now live.
>
> Think what this means. It means Banff will be part of heaven, and Rocky Mountain National Park. Toronto, especially Ontario Place, will be included. So will Miami and Montreal, Paterson and Vancouver. There is an outside chance for Grand Rapids.
>
> Of course, things will have to be purified and changed. It's hard to imagine smog and sleet and floods and urban decay in the new heaven and new earth. But it is this present earth that will be invaded by heaven—these forests, these mountains, this city and that one, these streams and rivers, lakes and lagoons. . . .
>
> Above all, Jesus Christ will be there. And everyone will be drawn to him as if by a magnet, for he is the center of the new heaven and new earth.

> **OPTION**
>
> If you had students describe the three things they would like best about heaven (see earlier option), talk about which of these things seem possible in view of the biblical givens.

- closed gates (no enemy to lock out).
- night.
- impurities or impure persons.

Present will be

- the holy city coming out of heaven and shining like a precious jewel.
- God himself dwelling with people and making everything new.
- the Lamb, Jesus Christ, who is also the lamp of heaven.
- the nations and their glory and honor.
- the kings of the earth and all their splendor.
- those whose names are written in the Lamb's book of life.

Ask if students have any comments or additional questions about the new heaven and the new earth, discussing as time permits.

Closing

For your closing prayer of praise, we suggest that students read Revelation 5:12, 13b, 14b, in unison:

"Worthy is the Lamb, who was slain,
to receive power and wealth and wisdom and strength
and honor and glory and praise!
To him who sits on the throne and to the Lamb
be praise and honor and glory and power, for ever and ever! Amen."

> **OPTION**
>
> Make photocopies and read responsively the following excerpts from the last two sections of *Our World Belongs to God*, (57-58) a contemporary testimony of the Christian Reformed Church:
>
> We long for that day
> when Jesus will return as triumphant king,
> when the dead will be raised
> and all people will stand before his judgment.
> We face that day without fear,
> for the Judge is our Savior.
> Our daily lives of service aim for the moment
> when the Son will present his people to the Father.
> Then God will be shown to be true, holy, and gracious.
> All who have been on the Lord's side will be honored,
> the fruit of even small acts of obedience
> will be displayed. . . .
>
> With the whole creation
> we wait for the purifying fire of judgment.
> For then we will see the Lord face to face.
> He will heal our hurts,
> end our wars,
> and make the crooked straight. . . .
> God will be all in all,
> righteousness and peace will flourish,
> everything will be made new,
> and every eye will see at last
> that our world belongs to God!
> Hallelujah! Come, Lord Jesus!

> **OPTION**
>
> If your students are interested, you may want to schedule an extra session and take Pastor Lew's suggestion to invite a guest speaker from a dispensational church. He or she could briefly present the premillennialist view of the end times and then handle any questions the students have. Ask your students to come prepared with some questions, and be sure to brief your guest on what the students have already learned. This could be a great opportunity for a friendly exchange of views by Christians from different traditions.

WHAT WE BELIEVE
SESSION 22

Being Distinctively Reformed

SCRIPTURE

Genesis 17:7; Psalm 8:1; 24:1; John 3:16; Romans 12:2; 1 Corinthians 10:31; Ephesians 1:4-5; 2:8; 2 Timothy 3:16; James 1:27

BELGIC CONFESSION

No specific references in today's session.

PURPOSE

Today's video describes what it means to be Calvinistic and Reformed in the broader context of Christianity. After explaining what being "Reformed" or "Calvinistic" ought not to suggest, Pastor Lew identifies ten characteristics that it does suggest: (1) believing Jesus is our Savior and Lord; (2) interpreting Christianity as the Reformers did, especially John Calvin; (3) making Scripture foundational to our faith and life; (4) using certain statements of faith to summarize biblical teachings; (5) emphasizing the sovereignty of God; (6) emphasizing the decrees of God; (7) living a disciplined Christian life; (8) reforming, rethinking old ideas and actions; (9) seeing history as one piece, united by the covenant of grace; (10) living with a "world-and-life-view."

After today's session, your students should have a better understanding of what it means to be Calvinistic or Reformed. They should be able to explain this in their own words, including at least some of the ten ideas (mentioned above) in their explanations. They should be able to list two or three specific ways that being Reformed affects their daily lives.

PERSPECTIVE

In the last century, the little community of Vriesland, Michigan, was the center of a debate over religious issues among Dutch Calvinists in that state. My ancestors were in the middle of it. Their passion was to be faithful to Scripture and to Reformed principles. After battling unbelief in Europe, migration to America gave them freedom to cultivate a Reformed lifestyle, and they applied themselves to it with diligence. I observed this as a youngster and had my impressions confirmed later in translating the consistory minutes of the Vriesland Reformed Church.

What does it mean to be Reformed? The following statement, although incomplete and imperfect, is an attempt to stimulate thinking about this question.

> To be Reformed is to believe in the sovereignty of the one true God who has manifested himself and his purpose for salvation in the Old and New Testaments; and, in spite of their sinful rebellion, has justified his covenant

people by grace through faith in Jesus Christ, and has sanctified them by the Holy Spirit, so that they seek to live unto him according to his will as expressed in his law. It means to believe in an ordered church, which ministers the Word and sacraments as true means of grace; to endeavor to apply Christian principles to every area of life; and to witness everywhere that the Lord reigns, that he calls all people to repentance and faith, and that someday all will appear before his judgment seat.

Central to Reformed theology is an idea found in both Luther and Calvin. That idea, *coram Deo* (that we live always in God's presence), was the heart of Calvin's theology and life. Living *coram Deo* means being ever conscious of God's presence and a call to live for him. It means accepting the mandate and privilege of consecrating ourselves to God, personally and socially. For he not only commands but he also empowers, and his resources are infinite. This commitment and power need to be manifest in the world today, as they were in the sixteenth century.

In a book called *The Faith of the Church*, I tried to trace the historical development of major doctrines from a Reformed perspective. After showing that Calvin accepted much in the theological tradition of the church before him, I defined his contribution to Christendom as "order and the Holy Spirit." By inheritance and training John Calvin emphasized both of these concepts. He saw salvation as the restoration of order, and he wrote widely on order in creation, church, state, and the Christian life. The Reformed churches adopted Calvin's belief that order is given by the Holy Spirit, and that sin disrupts order. Hence, we must be continually reforming, as the video tells us, so that we become conformed to the image of Christ.

Being distinctively Reformed, then, is not just a commitment to a system of theology or church government, as important as these are, but something more subtle and more profound. It is an active, faithful response to God's self-revelation. John T. McNeill finds it in a "type of piety familiar in the old Calvinism and once distinctive of it." He continues:

> This is a piety not much identified with peculiar words and rites of worship. It is characterized by a combination of God-consciousness with an urgent sense of mission. The triune God, Sovereign Creator, Redeemer, and Comforter, is an ever-present reality through both prosperity and disaster. Guilt is real, but it is submerged under grace. The Calvinist may not know how it happens; he may be a very simpleminded theologian; but he is conscious that God commands his will and deed as well as his thought and prayer. This is what makes him a reformer and a dangerous character to encounter on moral and political issues. He is a man with a mission to bring to realization the will of God in human society. . . . When he knows what is God's will, and how it is to be translated into action of the hour, he will espouse it with courage, energy, and tenacity. God has not given him the spirit of fear (*The History and Character of Calvinism,* pp. 433, 436ff.).

PROCEDURE

Review Quiz

1. false (No passage explicitly predicts a seven-year tribulation.)
2. true
3. false (We regard the thousand years as symbolic of completeness or wholeness.)
4. true
5. true
6. true
7. false (We will live with God and Jesus on the renewed earth.)
8. false (It was made between God and Abraham.)
9. true
10. true

Video Presentation

You'll notice that Pastor Lew suggests stopping the video (early on, just after the Bible Trivia) to have students jot down what they think "Reformed" or "Calvinistic" means. If you have time, distribute notecards and give students a minute or two to jot down their ideas; but don't be surprised if they don't have any—many adults wouldn't know how to answer this question! After sharing some responses, turn the video back on.

To help your students focus on one aspect of "being Reformed" at a time, we suggest you stop the video after each of Pastor Lew's descriptions of the ten characteristics. Discuss the question he just commented on, then return to the video and the next characteristic and question.

Video Discussion Guide

Each of today's discussion questions focuses on one of the traits of being Reformed or Calvinistic as presented on the video. We suggest that students look up the supporting Scripture passages before writing their answers.

1. **What's the first and most important thing you should say to someone who asks you what it means to be Reformed or Calvinistic? (See John 3:16; Ephesians 2:8.)**

    As Pastor Lew says, we have to start by saying that we are Christians, that Jesus is our Savior and the Lord of our lives. That's foundational to anything else we might say.

2. **As Calvinists, we interpret Christianity as the Reformers did, especially John Calvin. So we ought to know something about the man whose ideas helped shape our faith tradition. Identify the following:**

> **TIP**
> Today's session has ten questions and could run a bit long. You may want to skip the quiz to give you enough time for discussion. Also, if you find yourself running out of time, do not look up the Scripture passages listed for each question (Pastor Lew refers to many of these passages on the video.

> **OPTION**
> Assign one or more of the ten questions to each class member, asking each person to listen carefully for the answer to the assigned question. After the video, have each person look up the supporting Scripture passages, jot down an answer, and report that answer to the class for further discussion.

> **OPTION**
> Take a moment to deal with Pastor Lew's presentation of the caricature of Calvinists as dour, dull, stuffy persons. Do your students feel this way themselves? Do they hear something similar from their non-Reformed friends at school or elsewhere? Do they agree with Pastor Lew that these are stereotypes, that any faith tradition can be either dull or exciting?

> **OPTION**
> Encourage your students to memorize John 3:16 and/or Ephesians 2:8 as summaries of the gospel.

- **when Calvin lived**
- **the city Calvin reformed**
- **the famous book Calvin wrote**
- **how Calvin's influence spread**
- **churches today that are "Calvinistic"**

John Calvin was a scholar, writer, theologian, pastor, and civic leader. Although the video does not give this information, he lived from 1509-1564 (Luther began the Reformation in 1517). As the leading citizen and preacher of Geneva, Calvin helped apply the ideas of the Reformation to that city. Although he wrote more than ninety books, including commentaries on the books of the Bible, Calvin's greatest book is *The Institutes of the Christian Religion.* This book explains the biblical truths of the Reformation in an orderly way.

Calvin's influence spread throughout Europe and the entire world by means of his books and the students who attended his school in Geneva. Some of these students began churches in other countries; for example, John Knox started a church in Scotland that eventually became known as the Presbyterian Church.

"Calvinistic" churches today include Reformed churches (such as the Christian Reformed Church and the Reformed Church in America) and many Presbyterian churches. Explain that these churches generally interpret the Bible according to the thinking of Calvin (and other Reformers).

Be sure students understand that the ideas presented in the remainder of the session were those taught by Calvin (and some of the other Reformers as well).

> **OPTION**
>
> Duplicate the chart at the end of this session and distribute it to your students. The chart is a "family tree" of churches that will help your group understand how the "Reformed" branch of Christianity fits into the total picture (Pastor Lew mentions this briefly at the beginning of today's session).

3. **Like all true churches, Reformed churches place a high value on Scripture (see 2 Timothy 3:16). What evidence do you see in your congregation and around you that the Bible is crucial to our faith and our daily living?**

   Before discussing this question, note how Scripture testifies to its own importance, inspiration, and usefulness in 2 Timothy 3:16.

   Our preaching, our Bible studies, and our personal and family devotions all point to the central place the Bible has among us. More importantly, our daily lives should show that we take God's Word seriously enough to live by its principles. Do your students sense all these things happening in your congregation and in their families?

> **TIP**
>
> Please adapt this question and answer to your denomination and congregation.

4. **Calvinism is marked by holding to certain creeds and confessions that summarize biblical teachings from the Reformed perspective. Identify your church's creeds and confessions. Why are they necessary?**

Pastor Lew mentions three confessions held by the Christian Reformed Church and the Reformed Church in America: the Heidelberg Catechism, the Canons of Dort, and the Belgic Confession. In common with many other Christian churches, the Christian Reformed Church also recognizes the Apostles' Creed, the Nicene Creed, and the Athanasian Creed. In more recent years, it has written a fresh statement of faith called *Our World Belongs to God: a Contemporary Testimony.* And the Reformed Church in America has written a statement called "Our Song of Hope." These statements do not have creedal or confessional status but are recommended for use by the churches.

Pastor Lew suggests one reason why creeds and confessions are needed (to help people find their way through the Bible). Ask your group if they can think of other reasons as well.

> **TIP**
> You may want to show the group where to locate your church's creeds and confessions, if you suspect they don't know.

5. **One idea that distinguishes Calvinists from, say, Lutherans or Baptists or Methodists, is our emphasis on the sovereignty of God. When you think of the awesome power and supremacy of God, what comes to mind? How should God's sovereignty make us feel? (See Psalm 8:1; Psalm 24:1.)**

    Let students suggest places where they see God's sovereignty in action. Most will probably describe some sign of God's power in creation, such as the awesome power of a thunderstorm. Others may point to God's steady day-to-day care for everything he created, including us.

    Knowing that our God is in control of all things should give us a strong sense of awe and security.

6. **Calvinism stresses God's decrees, including *election* and *predestination*. What do these terms mean and how does believing them help us? (See Ephesians 1:4-5.)**

    It's been a long time since that lesson on election, so you may have to help students recall that election is simply God's choice to save some of the human race. "For he chose us in him before the creation of the world . . ." (Eph. 1:4).

    Predestination refers to all of God's decreeing and planning. As Pastor Lew says in today's video, "Things don't just happen by chance."

    These ideas comfort us by reminding us that God is in control of our salvation. Once he has chosen us, he will not let us slip away. Everything that happens to us is under God's control. As Pastor Lew says, we can "let God take care of the problems while we get to work and do what the Lord wants us to do."

7. **Calvinists believe in living disciplined Christian lives with definite standards and rules (see James 1:27). Give some examples of this from your own life. How can this kind of disciplined living help Christians?**

    Listen to some student examples and opinions here. Your teens know that we all need rules and boundaries. We need to learn how to live in the world without becoming like the world.

> **OPTION**
> You may also want to discuss how rigid rules and undue concern to stay "unpolluted by the world" can lead to legalism or an unhealthy isolation.

SESSION 22 • WHAT WE BELIEVE

You may find helpful these remarks by Cornelius Plantinga, Jr., in *A Sure Thing:*

> Our lives are firm and stable when we are disciplined by the law (of God). People can depend on us. They know we won't lose our Christian shape when forces push against us or pull on us. People can predict ahead of time that we will not lie or steal. They can depend on us to show reverence for God and respect for parents.
>
> But we must also be able to flex a little. Sometimes laws and rules cannot be our final answer. We need in us a person—a living, guiding person to inspire us with energy and enthusiasm for vital Christian living. For this we have in us the very Spirit of Christ (p. 285).

8. **Calvinists are a "reforming" people—that is, we test our ideas and practices (see Romans 12:2) against what the Bible teaches. Give an example that shows how your congregation or denomination is reforming. What is being evaluated or changed or initiated?**

   You may need to help your students find an example of an issue or program that your congregation is currently studying or evaluating or changing or initiating. For example, your congregation may be studying how it can do a better job of reaching its neighbors for Christ or your worship committee may be proposing changes in the liturgy. Be prepared to show that your congregation is not simply maintaining the status quo.

   On the denominational level, inform your class of some of the issues that are currently being discussed and/or acted upon. For instance, perhaps your denomination is publishing a new hymnal or updating a creed or writing a new creed. Or maybe it is redefining its stand on homosexuality or abortion. Possibly it is proposing some new program for expansion and growth.

   Point out that all "reforming" efforts are done (or ought to be done) in the light of God's Word. That's in line with the way Reformed churches came into existence: they "reformed" themselves according to God's Word, leaving a church that placed some of its own traditions and practices above that Word.

9. **Calvinists believe in a unified or covenantal view of history (see Genesis 17:7). What does this mean?**

   Students should remember from the last couple of sessions that Calvinists view history as one piece or as a straight line, unified by God's unchanging, covenant promise to always be our God if we respond in obedience and faith.

10. **Most Calvinists have what's called a "world-and-life-view." We'll look at this more closely next week. For a clue about what it means, look up 1 Corinthians 10:31.**

    Pastor Lew says very little about this on today's video. The passage cited says that everything we do should be dedicated to God's glory. Tell your group that this means that all of life—work, leisure, sports, politics, science, marriage, the family, and so on—is to be lived for the glory of God. More on this next time.

By way of summarizing today's session, have students think about how being a Calvinist affects—or could affect—their everyday lives. In other words, "So what?" So what if we believe these ten things? What difference will that make in my life?

Ask your students to jot down (perhaps on the flip side of the notecards used earlier in the session) two or three specific ways that being Reformed affects or could affect their daily lives. Sample their responses as time permits.

Closing

Ask students to say sentence prayers of thanks for one aspect of their congregation or denomination that they really appreciate.

> **OPTION**
>
> Take turns reading the prayer of Jesus for all believers (John 17:20-26).

> **OPTION**
>
> Read responsively the following section from *Our World Belongs to God* (43):
>
> We grieve that the church—
> which shares one Spirit, one faith,
>   one hope,
> and spans all time, place, race, and
>   language
> has become a broken communion in a
>   broken world.
> When we struggle for the purity of the
>   church
> and for the righteousness God
>   demands,
> we pray for saintly courage.
> When our pride or blindness blocks
> the unity of God's household,
> we seek forgiveness.
> We marvel that the Lord gathers the
>   broken pieces
> to do his work,
> and that he blesses us still
> with joy, new members,
> and surprising evidences of unity.
> We commit ourselves to seeking and
>   expressing
> the oneness of all who follow Jesus.

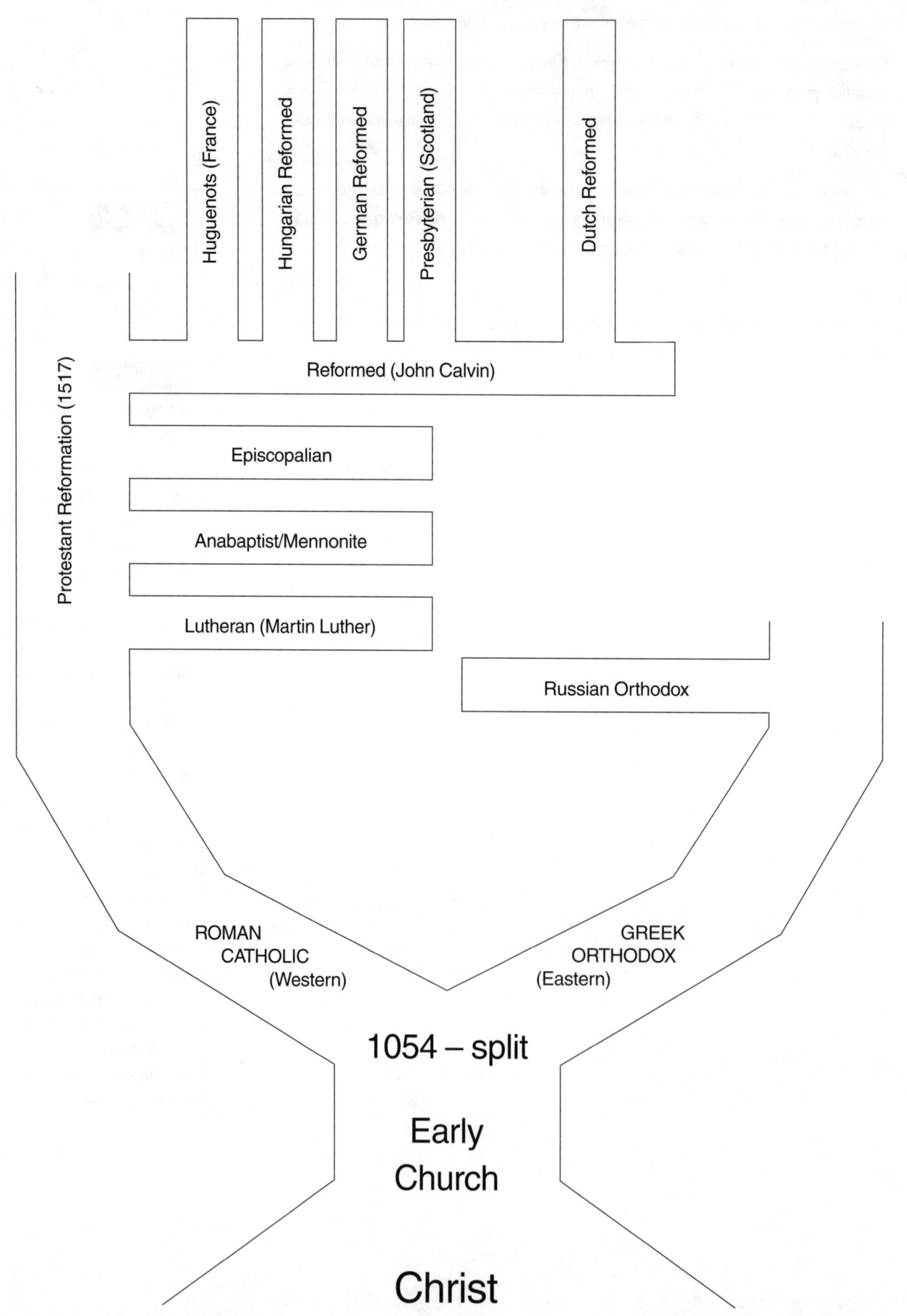

WHAT WE BELIEVE
SESSION 23

Living as a Christian

SCRIPTURE

Romans 12:2; 1 Corinthians 10:31

BELGIC CONFESSION

No references in today's session.

PURPOSE

In today's video, Pastor Lew focuses on the "world-and-life-view" of Calvinism and discusses the question "What does it mean to live as a Christian in the world?" He then presents six answers or approaches:

- What would Jesus do?
- Bible verse approach
- Opposition mode
- Common-sense method
- Love is the answer
- Understanding and transforming the world (world-and-life-view)

While all the approaches have strengths and weaknesses, this last is the one that's typical of Calvinism, says Pastor Lew. Next week's session will explore this approach in more detail. It will also discuss profession of faith.

After today's session, your students will have a better understanding of how they, as Christians, can relate to the world around them. They should be able to explain and evaluate each of the six approaches described in today's video, identifying the strengths and weaknesses of each approach.

PERSPECTIVE

God is the Lord of life; all of life belongs to God. Reformed Christians, among others, try to put this belief into practice. Thus we talk about a world-and-life-view in which faith is relevant to every area of life and has practical consequences for all activity. Abundant support for this idea is found in Scripture (for example, see 1 Cor. 10:31; Rom. 12:1-2; Col. 3:1-17). Dogmatics leads to ethics. "That truth is in order to goodness; and that the great touchstone of truth is its tendency to promote holiness" is the expressed presupposition of the polity of Presbyterianism, a presupposition that is etched deeply into the life of the Reformed churches. Orthodoxy and orthopraxis complement each other; that is, believing the correct doctrines goes hand in hand with practicing the right conduct. Calvin's writings clearly demonstrate this principle—he frequently denounced "empty speculations" and had great practical interest in people's daily lives. The principle is also evident in the Heidelberg Catechism, with its emphasis on the "benefit," "advantage," or "help" that we ought to receive from each article of our faith. The Christian's life is to be lived before the face of God; the catechism, like the Bible, should serve that end.

"Calling" or vocation is a theological concept that helps articulate what it means to live before the face of God. When Luther became convinced that in God's eyes the work of monks is no more important than that of farmers or homemakers, the doctrine of the universal priesthood of all believers was born.

Calvin embraced this teaching and gave it a large place in his writings and practice in Geneva. We exist not for ourselves but for God, and we find our true humanity only when we know God and live in relation to God. Then life is full of meaning, for we live it unto God. This teaching, which was revolutionary in the sixteenth century, is still revolutionary today at a time when humanity occupies the center of the stage and God exists, if at all, for the sake of humanity.

Living as Christians means that we are justified (accepted by God) by the grace of Christ and that we carry on from day to day by the power of the Holy Spirit.

Once we believe that, the question that looms before us is, How we are to live as Christians in a non-Christian world? Reformed people take that question seriously. Their answer is that we live as Christians by the power of the Holy Spirit. Through the Spirit we live as "monks-in-the-world"; Christ works in us through his Spirit to transform culture. The "impossible" becomes possible by the power of God. How can love prevail in a world bedeviled by hatred? Only by the power of the Holy Spirit. Jesus says that we are to love our enemies and pray for those who persecute us. How is this possible? Through the power of the Spirit, as we see in the history of the martyrs.

Clearly, Christian ethics differ from any other kind. In non-Christian ethics, say those of Immanuel Kant, we find maxims, rules for living—maxims devoid of power. Christian ethics are based on the power of Christ: the forgiveness of sins through the work of Christ, so that we can make a new beginning; the example of Christ; and the motivation of the Holy Spirit. The key to doing what we should be doing—transforming society—is having Christ's "incomparably great power," as Paul puts it, within us. The same power that raised Jesus from the dead (Eph. 1:19-20) is given us by the Holy Spirit; the strength of Calvinism is the proclamation of the Spirit's presence and power in the lives of God's people. Our calling is to offer our hearts to the Lord. However, human nature being what it is, we cannot do it on our own. With the mighty power that is given us we become able, and thus we glorify God.

Besides the help of God's Spirit, we are given the example of the Lord Jesus Christ and all the counsel, advice, admonitions, and commandments of the Word of God. To some, these latter may seem odious and to immature Christians burdensome, but they are, in fact, a blessing. Our heavenly Father did not speak all this for evil but for our good. His statutes are not fetters that bind us but liberators of our lives. They show us how we must live if there is to be any blessing. When, by grace, we have learned this lesson, we can say with the psalmist: "Oh, how I love your law! I meditate on it all day long" (Ps. 119:97).

PROCEDURE

Review Quiz

1. that Jesus is our Savior and Lord (or that we love Jesus, follow him, and so on)
2. John Calvin; Geneva
3. Scripture or the Bible
4. creeds or confessions
5. sovereignty
6. God's choosing to save some of the human race
7. disciplined or ordered or regulated
8. change or reform
9. glory
10. thousand

VIDEO PRESENTATION

Before showing today's video, ask your group to make a list of things they consider to be in the realm of the "sacred" and things they consider to be in the realm of the "secular" or non-religious. Put their ideas on your board or on a sheet of newsprint (save to use later in the session). A sample list follows:

Sacred
- church
- hymns
- Bible study
- prayers
- meditation
- the soul

Secular
- money
- work
- cars
- sex
- entertainment, sports
- the body

Don't tell the class (yet) that Calvinists generally resist dividing the world into neat "sacred" and "secular" columns; instead, just say that today Pastor Lew will talk about the relationship between the sacred and the secular, the Christian and the world. Specifically, he'll answer the question "How are we supposed to live as Christians in today's world?"

This week we suggest stopping the video for discussion after each of the six approaches.

OPTION

Play the video all the way through, but first assign each approach to two or more students who are responsible for presenting that approach to the class.

Video Discussion Guide

How do we live as Christians in today's world? Imagine that you have a tough decision to make. As a senior in high school, you have to decide what college to attend. Your choices boil down to just two: a local Christian college or a university several hundred miles away from home. Let's further assume that the two choices are equally appealing. While there are obvious differences in size and location and attractions, both offer a good education and housing at about the same cost. What's more, you'll have friends at both institutions. So how do you decide?

Talk about how each of the six approaches outlined in today's video would help you (or not help you) decide what to do. Also talk about how each approach sees the relationship between the Christian and world. What are the strengths and weaknesses of each approach?

1. **What would Jesus do?**

   With this approach, we'd simply ask, What if Jesus were facing this situation? What would he do? Would he choose the Christian college because there he'd be assured of getting the proper understanding of the world and could associate with Christian students in a Christian environment? Or would he go to the secular university to test his faith through contact with a wider worldview? We might reason that Jesus himself was taught by Jewish rabbis in a synagogue setting—a very strict and controlled religious upbringing. Furthermore, he brought his message to the Jews first and then to the wider world. On the other hand, his ministry clearly extended to "the world," and he never hesitated to mingle with so-called worldly people.

   This approach tends to see the world through Jesus' eyes—not a bad thing to do, as Pastor Lew says. *Ask your students when they would find this view most helpful.* Perhaps its not especially helpful in situations like our case study, but more so in situations that present a clearly wrong or dangerous choice. It's helpful to ask, What would Jesus do? when, say, being tempted to view a morally shabby movie or to climb up the bumper of the jerk who just cut you off. But, as Pastor Lew says, the approach is limited by how we see Jesus.

2. **Bible verse approach**

   Using this approach, we'd look through the Bible for verses that might give specific guidance on the subject at hand. For instance, we might find a verse like John 15:19 (which says Christians do not belong to the world) and conclude that we ought not go to the secular university. Or maybe we'd run across Mark 15:16 (which tells us to go into all the world and preach the gospel) and conclude that we should be witnesses in the world of the university. Or we might read the parable of the Prodigal Son and conclude that leaving home can be risky!

   This approach sees the world through the eyes of Scripture, and that's good. We said just last week that God's Word is foundational to our faith and to Christian living. So obviously we need to consult it and study it as we live from

> **TIP**
>
> What Would Jesus Do (WWJD) was very big when this was written. If your students are unfamiliar with it, be prepared to give some details about WWJD—maybe bring a WWJD bracelet to class to show them. On next week's video, one of the young people giving her testimonial talks about her WWJD bracelet and what it means to her. Note that WWJD bracelets were meant not only as a guide for the conduct of the wearer but also as a witnessing tool.

day to day. However, looking for texts that tell us clearly what to do is generally not a good use of Scripture, as the examples given on the video illustrate. Rather, we should look to Scripture for general principles that guide our behavior. Then we should carefully and prayerfully apply those principles to specific situations.

3. **Opposition mode**

Those who take this approach assume that the spiritual and the worldly are two separate and opposing things. Spiritual things are good; secular things are not. As Christians therefore we should venture into the secular only when necessary and then only in moderation. In the situation presented in our case study, the decision to attend the Christian college would be a no-brainer. Why mess around with the world if you don't have to?

As Pastor Lew says, it's good to set our minds on things above, to spend time in prayer and Bible reading, church work, and other "spiritual" things. That's better than focusing on things like money, possessions, sex, and entertainment. That sort of emphasis can make us strong Christians who can readily tell the difference between right and wrong and who fight vigorously against evil.

Let your group suggest what's not so good about this view (Pastor Lew didn't go into this on the video, so they're on their own here). A big problem with hanging around only with people who are like us is that it can result in unhealthy isolation. We close ourselves off to new ideas, new ways of doing things. As a result, we may even not be very eager to reach out with the good news of salvation.

Ask your group if they can give any examples of this approach. Maybe they see some of this attitude in parents or other adults who strongly promote certain religious activities but who are highly suspicious of entertainment, science, politics, and the like. Such parents may express a strong desire to protect their children from the world. Christians holding this view may be exceptionally active in the fight against obvious evils in society (such as pornography or abortion).

4. **Common-sense method**

Adherents of this approach also divide life into the secular and the sacred, but they don't consider the world an evil place. In their view the sacred and the secular exist side by side; we should keep them separate, but we can live in the world in a "common sense" way. In other words, we've got to make sure that we are good "kingdom citizens" by our church attendance, prayer, Bible reading, and so on. But at other times and places we've got to be involved in the world in a "common sense" way. We're good Christians but also (and separately) good citizens. So the decision of whether to attend a Christian college or a secular university is simply a matter of "common sense." It would be perfectly OK to go the secular university as along as you also found time to be a good Christian by attending church each Sunday, reading the Bible daily, and so on.

OPTION

Ask your students how God's Word guides them in their daily living. How do they go about using the Bible in a responsible way—as a "lamp to their feet and a light to their path" (Ps. 119:105)? Perhaps one or two students can give examples of how God's Word has helped them deal with a difficulty of some kind in their lives.

TIP

In your discussion of this and the remaining approaches, remember to refer to the list of "sacred" versus "secular" your group drew up at the beginning of this session.

TIP

Ask your students if they know of any groups that take this view to the extreme. Perhaps they've heard about such groups as the Amish people in Indiana and Pennsylvania or the Hutterites of Western Canada and United States. These groups often do without such "worldly" conveniences as electricity and automobiles. The early Dutch settlers in Holland, Michigan, also attempted for a time to isolate themselves from the unfamiliar world around them.

5. Love is the answer

Those who take this approach recognize that the greatest commandment is loving God above all and loving our neighbor as ourselves (Matt. 22:37-40). The principle of love, then, governs *all* our actions—in both the sacred and secular domains. So in the situation presented in our case study we would ask which would show the greater love for God and for others: attending the Christian college or attending the secular university. We might, for example, argue that our decision to go to a college whose professors are Christians and whose philosophy is Christian would honor God more than going to a university that did not recognize God. And if our parents really wanted us to do attend a Christian college, that would be a clear way of showing that we love them. Of course, arguments could be made in the other direction as well.

Impress on your students that this "law of love'" is a beautiful biblical principle that should indeed be applied to all aspects of life. Trouble is, too often "love" gets reduced to "warm fuzzies" or just "doing what feels good." In the example Pastor Lew gives on the video, relying on "love" to govern one's behavior on a date can be a risky proposition!

6. Understanding and transforming the world (world-and-life-view)

This approach, held by Calvinists, teaches that life is not split into "sacred" and "secular" domains. Instead, life is one piece with many different parts (economics, politics, marriage, the family, education, and so on). Our task is first of all to look at God's creation and understand how God intends each part of it to function. Then we are to live all areas of our lives in a way that brings God glory (1 Cor. 10:31). When we see that a part of God's creation has been damaged, we set out to redeem or transform that part of creation as best we can, to the glory of God (Rom. 12:1-2). In a sense, then, everything we do is sacred, an act of worship to God.

So how would the Calvinist go about deciding whether to attend a Christian college or a secular university? There's no easy or right answer here, of course. But if we follow the two-fold task outlined above (understand, transform), the Calvinist would probably begin by doing some heavy thinking and reading about the purpose of higher education. We would surely ask which institution would best prepare us for understanding and transforming that part of God's world where we feel called to work.

The strength of Calvinism is that it doesn't divide life into two categories; it is holistic, affirming that all of life is sacred and can be redeemed. It is a positive approach that enrolls Christians in the wonderful work of realizing the rule of Christ over every part of life. Pastor Lew doesn't mention its snares, so let the group give their own ideas. One is that "transforming the world" is such a lofty ideal. It sounds pretentious, impossible (by way of answering this objection, be sure to mention the enabling role of the Holy Spirit—see Perspective). Another drawback is that working in the world always carries the danger of becoming

---

OPTION

This is heavy going, we know. But it's important and worth the time you'll need to help your students understand the "world-and-life-view" or "cultural mandate," as it's sometimes called. It's an approach advocated and practiced by Reformed or Presbyterian (Calvinistic) churches (we'll go into more detail on this next time). To bring this down to earth a bit, you could ask for examples of how Christians from your church or community are working to change some part of our world. For example, perhaps a church member is active in politics or in public education or in prison ministry or the entertainment field. Point out (again) that simply trying to live every part of our lives to God's glory is the heart of this approach. We don't have to be a politician or entertainer; we can work for God's glory at school, on our jobs, at home . . . everywhere.

part of it. Still another is that making culture what God wants it to be is hard work with few immediate rewards.

Summarize by inviting students to reflect on how they personally view their own relationship to the world. Ask if today's session has helped them to clarify their thinking. What significance, if any, does the whole matter have for their daily lives?

Closing

If time permits, have a couple of students read Romans 12:2 and 1 Corinthians 10:31 to the group.

Then invite each group member to pray silently for God's help in "transforming" one area of his or her life that's currently causing some difficulty or pain or temptation. Close the prayer time by thanking God for giving us a part in healing and restoring his world.

> **TIP**
> You should also point out that all the approaches we talked about today aren't limited just to reaching a decision. They are ways of living out the Christian life from day to day. The view that we hold affects the way we use our spare time, our attitude toward work, and much of what we say and do. By the way, don't be overly concerned if some of your students favor a view other than the Calvinistic one. Your goal here is to just explain the Calvinistic stance—and to get your students to do some reflecting on it. You don't need to make any converts.

> **OPTION**
> *Our World Belongs to God* expresses the "world-and-life-view" of Calvinism in many of its sections, especially sections 44-55. These touch on protecting life, living as male and female, serving Christ as singles and families, in our work, in science and technology, in politics, in public justice, and in working for peace. You may want to read some of these sections with your students.

> **OPTION**
> Here's an option for an extra session. What does it mean to "transform culture"? Suppose, for example, you invited a panel of several folks from your congregation to tell how they attempt to let their Christianity show at work, to affect change for the better on their jobs? It really doesn't matter what their job is—doctor, mechanic, grocery store clerk, teacher, fast-food worker, judge, student . . . try for a good variety in occupations and ages. Brief your panel on what you've taught about Calvinism and encourage your group to participate with questions.

WHAT WE BELIEVE
SESSION 24

Profession of Faith/Recommitment

SCRIPTURE
Mark 8:38; Romans 10:9; Philippians 4:8

BELGIC CONFESSION
No references in today's session.

PURPOSE
In this last session of Part Two and of the course, Pastor Lew reviews and gives examples of the Calvinistic view of the relationship between the Christian and the world. The remainder of the video discusses public profession of faith. Why should we profess our faith? First, God commands it. Second, we are never good enough ("ready") to profess our faith but should do so if we truly love the Lord. Third, it is hypocritical not to confess Christ when we believe in him. Fourth, we don't have to perfectly understand and completely accept all of the doctrines of a particular church before professing our faith. The video concludes with the testimonies of four teens and a "goodbye" from Pastor Lew.

After today's session, your students should be encouraged to consider professing their faith in Christ (if they've already taken that step, they'll be motivated to renew their commitment). They will be able to explain the necessity and the meaning of publicly professing their faith, critique reasons commonly given for waiting to profess faith, and evaluate their own walk with Jesus.

PERSPECTIVE
The Calvinistic world-and-life-view argues that there is no secular territory for Christians. All that God has made is sacred and bears a relationship to him. Sin has done great damage, but Christ has overcome sin and extends the effects of his redemption everywhere. He uses people who, as part of the "new creation" (2 Cor. 5:17), pray "your kingdom come, your will be done" and then help make that happen. Calvinists believe that with God's help, people become transformers of society.

To be a coworker with God in the struggle for good and against evil in this sin-sick but wonderful world, there must be an act of will, of commitment. The early church professed, *Credo: ergo confiteor*—I believe: therefore I confess. To be a confessor at that time meant possible death, but those Christians felt that they had to stand up and be counted out of loyalty to Christ.

Differences between the kingdom of God and the kingdom of evil may appear to be less openly hostile and more subtle and invisible today than they did in the first centuries of the church. But today's differences are just as real. That is why it is as important for disciples to declare themselves today as it was in the days of the Caesars. The intervening centuries have brought changes, but human nature remains the same, and the powers of darkness are as insidious as ever.

The Bible tells us that if we confess with our mouths that Jesus is Lord and believe in our hearts that God raised him from the dead, we will be saved (Rom. 10:9). Jesus says that he will acknowledge before his Father those who acknowledge him before other people, but he will deny before God those who deny him (Matt. 10:32-33; Luke 12:8-9). On another occasion he warned that on that great last day, when he comes with his angels, he will be ashamed of those who were ashamed of him (Mark 8:38; Luke 9:26).

Confessing Christ means identifying ourselves with him and his church. For your students it means a desire on their part to be on God's side in the war between God and the devil. All of us are identified with the persons and organizations to which we belong—family and friends, schools and clubs, this team and that society. Christians are also identified with Christ and his church. The persons and organizations we are identified with become a part of us in the measure to which we give ourselves to them. That holds true for life's highest priorities. Paul said that he was one with Christ (Gal. 2:20), and Christ identified himself with the church (Eph. 5:25-27; John 15:1-8). When we sincerely confess Christ as Savior and Lord, we identify ourselves with him. The King of kings, who so loved us that he became one of us and died on a cross for us, becomes our intimate friend. What a privilege!

PROCEDURE

Review Quiz

Here are the answers to today's true/false quiz (with false answers corrected).

1. true
2. false (The Bible usually provides general principles rather than specific advice on what to do in a given situation.)
3. true
4. true
5. false (Most important are loving God and loving our neighbor.)
6. true
7. true
8. true
9. false (Baptism and the Lord's Supper are the only two sacraments recognized by Reformed/Presbyterian churches.)
10. false (Reformed churches emphasize the sovereignty of God.)

OPTION

Invite students to jot down on a separate sheet of paper any questions they would like to discuss during today's final session (or later, in an additional session, if need be). Collect the questions and deal with them at some point in today's session.

OPTION

For variety's sake, you may want to try a different kind of review quiz today. Give students about five minutes to make up five true/false statements of their own. Three of the statements should be based on last week's session about how to live as a Christian in the world; two of the statements should be based on previous sessions. Students may use previous session guides, if available, but the questions should be their own. After writing their true/false statements, students should divide into pairs and ask each other their questions.

Video Presentation

Today's video has two distinct parts. In the first few minutes, Pastor Lew returns to the Calvinistic view of the world and gives examples of how that view works out in people's lives. The second part deals with profession of faith. You may want to stop the video after the first part for discussion of questions 1-2, then continue with the second part and questions 3-8.

Video Discussion Guide

1. **How do Calvinists view the world? What is our task in it?**

   Calvinists do not divide life into the sacred and the secular but see it as a whole. For Christians, all of life is sacred. Our task is to look for those parts of life that have become damaged and polluted by sin and attempt to transform them into what God intended them to be, to make them beautiful again. In so doing, we "do all for the glory of God."

2. **Pastor Lew gives some examples of ways that Christians are working to change some aspects of our society for the better. Give some additional examples that you've heard about or participated in. How have you or other Christians from your church or youth group or school attempted to "transform" some part of our society or world that needs healing?**

   Thinking about transforming the broken parts of our culture into something beautiful for Christ is a daunting task. Focusing on what your church or youth group has done (or is doing or plans to do) can do helps narrow the focus a bit. Your teens may cite such things as working in a food pantry, cleaning up a neighborhood or section of highway, tutoring a younger student, painting a house, protesting an unfair law, fighting racism or violence, or modeling good behavior at a hotly contested sports event.

3. **What reason for professing our faith does Romans 10:9 give?**

   This passage says that to be saved, we must confess with our mouth that Jesus is Lord and believe in our hearts that God raised him from the dead. The reason, then, for publicly confessing Christ is that God commands it in his Word.

4. **Pastor Lew implies that if we wait until we're "ready" to profess our faith, we'll never do so. Do you agree? Why or why not? What helped some of the teens on the video know that they were ready to take a stand for Jesus?**

   Invite your students to speak from their own experience. In one sense, "readiness" is important—obviously, we shouldn't confess our faith if we have no love for Jesus in our hearts. On the other hand, if we love the Lord and hesitate to confess his name because we realize we're still sinful, then it's time to take a stand for Jesus.

> **TIP**
>
> If most of your students have not yet publicly professed their faith, you may want to spend all the available time on this topic, using only questions 3-8. Today's video makes a strong but sensitive case for young believers to publicly profess their faith in Christ. When you discuss this topic in class, do so in a way that promotes open discussion and points kids to the Lord Jesus, who loves them and wants their love in return. Be sure to allow time to deal with question 8, which invites your students to talk about their personal spiritual journeys.

> **TIP**
>
> Tell the group that this "transforming" business needn't be all that complex. One of the simplest ways we can transform things that are tainted by sin is to start with our own lives and then look at the world around us. We can learn to say no to sin and to focus on "whatever is true, whatever is noble, whatever is right, whatever is pure, whatever is lovely, whatever is admirable" (Phil. 8:4). Simply understanding what God wants of us at school, on the job, and at home, and then doing our best to accomplish that, is a way of transforming our culture and glorifying God.

SESSION 24 • What We Believe

The teens on the video suggested a number of things that signaled to them that they were ready:

- awareness that the Holy Spirit was working in their lives
- realization that prayer is "for real"
- a sense of guidance from God's Word
- feeling the need to tell everybody they love Jesus
- feeling like part of the church
- a sense that "Jesus is there for me"

5. **Which is more offensive to you: people who have publicly professed their faith but who don't live as Christians or people who believe in Jesus but who won't publicly confess his name? Why?**

Pastor Lew suggests that both actions are hypocritical. Your students will surely see the hypocrisy in saying that you love Jesus but then living from day to day as if you don't. Such deceptive behavior may even discourage others from professing their own faith in Christ. Remind those who have professed their faith of the importance of living it.

Do your students agree that believing but not confessing can also be hypocritical? They may feel that the comparison is off the mark—after all, young Christians may have valid reasons for waiting to profess their faith. But help them understand that both actions can be offensive. "If anyone is ashamed of me and my words in this adulterous and sinful generation, the Son of Man will be ashamed of him when he comes in his Father's glory with the holy angels," Jesus warns (Mark 8:38).

6. **Which, if any, teaching(s) of the church do you feel uneasy or unclear about? Should these feelings keep you from professing your faith? Why or why not?**

Here's an opportunity to let students talk about some of their doctrinal doubts and reservations, if they have any. Assure them that it often takes time to understand and appreciate all the teachings of the church. (Of course, if we can't accept the Trinity or Christ's atonement or the resurrection, our faith has little or no content.) But as Pastor Lew says, the most important thing is that we love God.

7. **Did any of the comments from the teens on the video help you in some way? Offend you? Raise a question for you? Express your own feelings? Please explain.**

This question gives your group a chance to react to the teens on the video. You may hear some criticisms, but we hope you'll also hear some acknowledgment of being touched by a comment or example. The teens on the tape sincerely

---

> **OPTION**
>
> One additional aspect of professing one's faith that you may want to talk about is how your students feel about being part of a congregation. Are they growing spiritually? Are they comfortable with the people? If they have some reservations, should that keep them from professing their faith within that congregation? Why or why not? Invite your students' opinions. Comment that if we wait to find a congregation that fits us just right, we may be passing up some opportunities to serve. And we may be giving up the possibility of really getting to know and love the people in our own congregation.

and honestly express their faith in Jesus—while acknowledging that commitment isn't always easy and doesn't end all their struggles.

8. **This is the last question in this course—and the most important. *Where are you today in your own walk with Jesus?*** **Share as little or as much as you wish. If you've professed your faith, you may want to say what it means to you today. If you've not done that, you may want to talk about your reasons for waiting. The important thing is to express your feelings honestly and sincerely.**

   Talking about their personal spiritual journeys poses no threats for some teens but is highly intimidating to others. Keep participation voluntary. Encourage honesty, even if it means saying that right now God seems very distant and confessing faith in him isn't even on the radar.

   You'll notice that we've put the emphasis on spiritual journeys, keeping talk about profession of faith secondary. The goal is to have a time of meaningful sharing, not to push students to profess. Of course, if some of your students have professed their faith, their testimony could be very helpful and encouraging to other students who, for whatever reasons, are waiting. And if some of the students want to share their reasons for waiting, that too could be helpful to the others. Some may feel they still don't know enough or aren't sure. Others may resent parental pressures or may be holding back for reasons they don't want to share. Let them know it's their decision; no one in the church will pressure them into doing something they are not ready to do.

Closing

Conclude this final session with a time of silent reflection. Have your students close their eyes and think about their spiritual life and their relationship with God.

If they've professed their faith, invite them to pray for courage to keep confessing his name with their words and their lives. If they haven't professed their faith, invite them to pray silently for God's guidance. Close the prayer yourself, thanking God for each young person and for the time he's given you together.

Note: Since this is the final session, you may want to talk with your students about what they liked and disliked about this course. And please pass their comments—and yours—along to us. You can reach us at 1-800-333-8300 or e-mail us at editors@crcpublications.org. Thank you.

TIP

If you're willing, tell the group that you're available to talk with anyone on this topic or anything related to it (make your phone number available and give a specific time when you can be reached). You may also want to make a handout showing the various steps your congregation follows in the process of profession of faith.

OPTION

If your class is large, divide into small groups for this final question. Some students may be more willing to share honestly with their peers than with you.

OPTION

As a summary of the course, say the Apostles' Creed together.